Meeting Mystery, Holding Hope

October 2008

Doing Theology at Pilgrim Place

Volume III: 2007-2008

Edited by Paul Kittlaus and Pat Patterson

Wasteland Press
Shelbyville, KY USA
www.wastelandpress.net

Meeting Mystery, Holding Hope
Doing Theology at Pilgrim Place: Volume III
Edited by Paul Kittlaus and Pat Patterson

First Printing–September 2008
ISBN: 978-1-60047-242-8

Cover photo by Sioux Bally Maloof

Printed in the U.S.A.

CONTENTS

Introduction

So here we are, completing our third annual circle of Doing Theology. Stimulated and enriched, we have been remembering and reflecting, analyzing and searching for vision, grieving and finding comfort, questioning and celebrating. We stand at the Pilgrim Place flagpole and pray for peace; we make artistic and useful crafts; we gather for exposure and discussion of national and global issues; we cherish and support our families near us and afar; we participate in our retirement community's decisions and witness. We bring all the currents of our lives to bear on the task of Doing Theology.

Our lives are bounded by mystery. The beginning and the ending are full of wonder. Birth and death, like bookends, hold the outside limits of our being. But all along the way we confront mystery--in encounter with the Divine, in delight of the beloved, in circles of family and friends, in confrontation with tragedy, in hunger for justice, in expression of creativity, in interdependence with all the earth's creatures, in awe of the universe.

Reflecting on our lives, we hold up to the light their beauty and sadness, their moments of celebration and despair, their dead ends and their amazing new beginnings. In sharing with each other, our journeys take on more profound meaning. We are embraced by each other's insights and compassionate listening. We receive ourselves again as gifts of the Mystery.

Our aspirations for a just and peaceful world bring together tragic uncertainty and fragile hope. In the midst of evil and destruction and war, we can still imagine that "another world is possible" and that ultimate reality is aimed at the welfare of all people and all creation. This unconquerable spirit pervades all that we are and do. In our personal and public lives we are comforted and strengthened and encouraged to go on.

Even when we struggle like Jacob with God and are wounded by tangling with mysterious angels,[1] we grow beyond ourselves into new dimensions of selfhood and community. And we continue our search for clearer understanding, for wiser resources to meet daunting challenges, and for deeper connection with our ancestors and our

---

[1] Genesis 32:24-31.

contemporaries and generations to come. We say like one centuries ago, "Lord, I believe; help my unbelief."[1] And we keep on dreaming of a more perfect union, a more just and caring world.

Doing theology together gives us companions and their exquisite insights for this lifelong challenge. We invite you to join us. Your reading and pondering widen the circle of energy and hope. And with these basic elements we believe that God, our ultimate Mystery, continues the work of creation and redemption.

Appreciation: We salute each of the presenters and writers. But we give special thanks to Don Chatfield, who has corrected and shaped our manuscripts for publication. For Volume III, as well as for Volumes I and II, his skillful and critical attention has been an essential contribution and a genuine blessing.

Paul Kittlaus and Pat Patterson, *editors*
Claremont, California
Summer 2008

---

[1] Mark 9:24.

At the Flagpole[1]
Paul Kittlaus
September 19, 2007

If it's Monday
This must be the flagpole
I keep the vigil
I stand with those
Whom God has given hope
To counter the news
Of the day

If it's Thursday
This must be the flagpole
The sun bakes from above
Or the grey clouds weep
Their tears
I keep the vigil
With those out of their minds
Crazy with love for the world
Crying for the bombs falling
The people dying
The children crying
The homes in rubble
The mothers who stumble
On their broken dreams
Of a home and family
Of Peace in the land
Of sleep in the quiet night
Of awakening to a new dawn of hope

If it's Monday
This must be the glad pole

---

[1] Since the military response by the US in Afghanistan soon after 9/11, and throughout the Iraq war (responses many of us found wrong), a group of residents has gathered twice a week at the campus flagpole for a silent prayer vigil prior to our noon meal together. We each bring whatever prayers for justice and peace are on our hearts. At the close of our time together we share God's peace with a handshake or a hug and a few words.

Elevating a flag to the winds
A symbol of a nation I love
And a symbol of destruction
For that mother

If it's Thursday
This must be the flagpole
This must be the vigil
These must be the company
Of brothers and sisters
Reminding ourselves
Of who we are
By this silent time
This vigil
This act of defiance
Against the news of the day

If this is Monday or
If this is Thursday
And if it is noon
It is time for the ritual
Of silence
Of standing before my God
In my appeal for forgiveness
For the world we are leaving our children
How could I have failed so miserably
To build a world of justice
For them to inhabit

If this is Monday or
If this is Thursday
I go to the flagpole
Take my place in the circle
It has no political significance
Yet clearly I do it for myself
To remind myself who I am
And of the gospel that claims me

This must be the flagpole
I pray for my nation
And for the world God has given
And for all the suffering
For which I am responsible
Because I am a citizen
This must be the flagpole
The flagpole
Come Lord Jesus
Be our guest
At the flagpole
At the flagpole
On Monday
On Thursday
At the flagpole

On Still Looking for God
Larold Schulz
October 3, 2007

If only I knew where to find the Almighty, so I could approach the Judgment Seat! But if I go east, God isn't there; if I go west, I find nothing. When God is working up north, I can see no one; when God turns south, I don't even catch a glimpse.

Job 23:3, 8-9

Blessed are those whose hearts are clean: they will see God.

Matthew 5:8

For I was hungry and you fed me; I was thirsty and you gave me drink. I was a stranger and you welcomed me; naked and you clothed me. I was ill and you comforted me; in prison and you came to visit me.

Matthew 25:35-36

In Christopher Fry's verse-play *A Sleep of Prisoners*, David says to Adams, "Allow me to make an introduction. God; man. Man; God." But Adams knows better. He knows, perhaps too well, the difficulty, the agony, the frustration of keeping God in focus. He replies wistfully to David: "I wish it could be so easy."

If you are anything like me, you know all too well Adams' problem. We, too, wish it could be so easy. We wish we could know God more clearly, understand God's seemingly changeable ways more plainly, and feel more comfortable in our relationship. Like Job, we are often in deep trouble. We don't seem to be able to find God anywhere. At least not the cozy and comfortable God we learned about in Sunday school. We have real difficulty with the God who punishes sinners and rewards the righteous, certainly that can't be the God who lives in the heavens (with the stars) or "within" (near our heart). We, like Job, have times when we can't find God either in our past, in the present, or in space and time. No wonder Job's faith was shaken.

Job's friends kept telling him that he was suffering because of wrongdoing. God was punishing him, even if he couldn't remember what it was he had done. Job couldn't handle this. He had a difficult time dealing with an understanding of God that had to do with divine

4

retribution and even the possibility of alienation. Job was so honest about his feelings that he actually hurled defiant questions at God.

There have been times when I've had the same inclination. Times when life has treated me unjustly, or more often when others have been treated unjustly. There have been many times when I've wanted to ask the unseen God why there is so much injustice in the world, so much pain and poverty, so many tears. There have been so many wakeful nights, staring into the dark at 3:00 A.M., and wondering about it all. There have been times when I've actually thought that God is more like an enemy than a friend. That's what happened to Job. Before he could actually accept God as a friend, he had to think of God as an enemy.

Similarly, when Adam and Eve, in the biblical myth, tried to hide from God in the garden, they lost their sense of God's presence. When Abraham cried to heaven, "Shall not the Judge of all the earth do right?" he called into question God's fair play. When the Psalmist, like many prophets, complained, "How long, O God, how long?" he was unsure about God as a keeper of promises. Jesus had his own profound crises of faith, as when he wrestled with his destiny in the desert of temptation, and again in the Garden of Gethsemane, but particularly in the terrible cry of abandonment from the Cross, "My God, my God, why have you forsaken me?"

Obviously these matters are much on my mind these days. It hasn't always been that way. Throughout my life I really never gave them much thought. I think that in the back of my mind, God was in charge and ultimately everything would, to paraphrase Paul, "work out." In those days many of us were in exciting situations in which we could often see change for good actually happening. It was slow going but the process was often exciting and stimulating. As I often say to Donna, "I really felt as if I was doing something important then and my life was making a difference." I don't feel that way any more. It is now clear to me that the all "too small" God I once believed in is beyond my comprehension and recognition.

In my last sharing with this group I spoke about God being hidden. I quoted from Ignazio Silone's great novel, *Bread and Wine*, in which the hero, Pietro Spina, has become a revolutionary with a price on his head. Though formally in exile, he returns to Italy in disguise. Though now an atheist, he disguises himself as a priest, and he cannot resist visiting the old priest who first taught him so wisely and well. When the old priest speaks of the strange ways of the hidden God, Spina responds defensively:

'I lost my faith in God many years ago . . . It was a
religious impulse that led me into the revolutionary
movement, but, once within the movement, I gradually
rid my head of all religious prejudices . . .'

Today I must admit that, for me, the Bible is not just a book of
faith, it is a book of faith and doubt. It is a narrative that is
excruciatingly honest about struggles of persons seeking to come to
terms with what is "really real" when everything is crumbling around us
and what really can be counted on at the most difficult times of life, and,
yes, even death. When God seems remote, or maybe even "dead," the
Bible helps me wrestle with my doubts and fears because it contains
stories about how those who have gone before have attempted to handle
the doubts and fears of all their years. It's not meant to scold, or correct,
or tell us what to believe—as if you could command a drowning person
to swim or someone who is deeply confused to think clearly, or easily
transform doubt to trust.

So, here we are as a society, drowning, confused and doubting.
Here I am with malignant cancer and incurable neuropathy which saps
my energy and makes it difficult for me to do things that really seem
important. I don't fear death, I fear living. I fear that, in a sense, God is
hidden from me. Where I was once full of spirit and energy, I now feel
empty. Where I once sought light, now I feel more comfortable in
darkness. Where I used to love doing, engaging, leading, now I tend to
withdraw and back off.

I looked forward to retirement as a time when, at last, I would
have the time to become more involved in effective political action, the
time to utilize my organizational skills and creativity within a broad
range of groups working to change the systemic evils that are malignant
cancers in our society. I thought that there would be opportunities to
preach and teach. I dreamed of being able to "make a difference."

Instead, in the process of moving from of our former residence to
come to Pilgrim Place my kneecap fractured so I was, when I arrived
here, unable to function at "full speed." Then I soon learned that my
"style" or "size" or "loud voice" were off-putting to the "culture" of
Pilgrim Place. Apparently I was perceived as a "bull in a china shop"
which, in fact, I am when it comes to being up front and right out as a
"truth teller." This meant that my organizational and administrative
skills were not appreciated and this has led to much frustration. Then in
the difficult process of trying to get my knee replaced the lymphoma was

discovered, and with that my life has been turned upside down.

In many ways and at many times I have felt that God is hidden from me. If it weren't for Donna, many of you, my family, plus classical music, life would not be worth living. I understand better the biblical personages that tell of persons experiencing what they felt to be disconnection not only with their community, but also with God.

These experiences have led to considerable introspection, something I've not done before. I'm not a "navel gazer." I don't meditate, silence is threatening, and I have a hard time getting my head around "spiritual" exercises. However, every night I wake up and my mind races while I think of problems here and around the world and create scenarios about how I might be involved in helping change conditions. I find myself constantly trying to figure out what is "really real" and how God's will for my life might fit into some plan that could be put into practice.

I am reminded of the Rabbit in Margery Williams's wonderful story, *The Velveteen Rabbit*. Let me quote, at length, a portion of that story for the few of you who may not know it. The story is set in a child's nursery and the Rabbit and Skin Horse are stuffed animals.

> Rabbit was made to feel himself very insignificant and commonplace, and the only person who was kind to him at all was the Skin Horse. The Skin Horse had lived longer in the nursery than any of the others. He was so old that his brown coat was bald in patches and showed the seams underneath, and most of the hairs in his tail had been pulled out to string bead necklaces. He was wise, for he had seen a long succession of mechanical toys arrive to boast and swagger, and by-and-by break their mainsprings and pass away, and he knew that they were only toys, and would never turn into anything else. . . . 'What is REAL?' Asked the Rabbit one day, when they were lying side by side near the nursery fender, before Nana came to tidy up the room. 'Does it mean having things that buzz inside you and a stick-out handle?' 'REAL isn't how you are made,' said the Skin Horse. 'It's a thing that happens to you. When a child loves you for a long, long time, not just to play with, but REALLY loves you, then you become REAL.' . . . 'Does it happen all at once, like being wound up,' he

asked, 'or bit by bit?' 'It doesn't happen all at once,' said the Skin Horse. 'You become. It takes a long time. That's why it doesn't happen often to people who break easily, or have sharp edges, or who have to be carefully kept. Generally, by the time you are REAL, most of your hair has been loved off, and your eyes drop out and you get loose in your joints and very shabby. But these things don't matter at all; because once you are REAL you can't be ugly, except to people who don't understand.'

I'm fortunate that my mother and my wife Donna have made it possible for me to know that I am "real." Their caring, nurturing and forgiving love has served as prototypical human examples of God's caring, nurturing and forgiving love. Many others, some in this room, have also provided a sense of how God touches my life. The problem is, that in the anguish and frustration that each of us faces at some time in our lives, we tend to feel that God is absent.

After Elijah had dispatched the prophets of Baal at Mount Carmel and Ahab ran home to tell Jezebel about it, Elijah was so scared that he started running so he himself would not be killed. Even though he must have realized that God had something to do with the events at Carmel he felt that God was hidden from him and he'd better leave the area quickly. This story in the 18th and 19th chapters of 1 Kings states that Elijah sat under a broom tree and said to God, "It is enough, now take away my life." He then kept running for forty days and ended up hiding in a cave. At that cave God spoke to him saying, "Elijah, what are you doing here?" And then came an earthquake, wind, and fire, but God was not in any of these. Surely God was hidden. Then there was the sound of sheer silence and out of it Elijah heard again, "What are you doing here, Elijah?"

It is clear to me that I've been running. Away from . . . I know not what. I wish that I could stop and answer the question, "What am I doing here?" Frankly, I don't know. It is also clear that the earthquakes, winds, and fires going on everywhere in the world where there is violence and increasing suffering of the poor and powerless, continue while I hide in my cave here at Pilgrim Place. Not only is God hidden from me, I'm hiding from God.

God has always hidden from the world. God hid in a burning bush, in a cloud by day and a pillar of fire by night, in a baby born in a stable, in a Cross between two thieves on top of a garbage dump, and in an empty tomb. God hides, and in times like this, I'm not certain where to search. God is hidden, but God is at work. My difficulty is that if God works though people like you and me, I feel like I'm not doing my part.

That brings me back to Job. Job came to the realization that God does not always come at things from our point of view. God is not always on our side (thank goodness). But as in Job's case, God welcomes dialogue. If Gracie Allen was right, we are the ones putting periods where God has only placed commas. In the end Job found his answer to faith only when he gave up trying to justify and understand and instead let his protest come out fully instead of suppressing it. Only in that way could he find an answer that was his and not someone else's. Job recognized the "still speaking" God.

Perhaps what I am seeking is that "still speaking" God who is always above whatever thought processes or concepts I can marshal. A God who draws us near in love in God's own time and way, perhaps just as we are about to give up. Job's friends thought they had God in their pockets. They had all the neat answers, and they repeated them over and over again. But that doesn't work when life pushes us hard. Job learned that the official creedal formulas of that day were irrelevant to his situation. Dogma is a straight jacket, whether it is from the right or the left, from the conservative or the liberal. He knew that in crying out he would be judged a heretic or blasphemer. But he cried out. In so doing he found a vital and living faith. He discovered that it is under pressure, at moments of extremity, when all familiar props have been knocked out from under us, when our lives have gone bankrupt, if we are willing to acknowledge it, that God is given a chance to come out of hiding. God comes to us in a moment that God chooses—in times of distress, in seasons of despair, even in moments of defiance. It is then that God may be closer than at any other time.

Samuel H. Miller, in *The Dilemma of Modern Belief*, put it this way: "When, like the Prodigal Son, we do come to ourselves (as Job did), I do not know how your fences will be shattered, your labels burned, or your pride and pretensions humbled, but I do know that the Realm of God is still in the process of becoming, even amidst the desperate violence of humans, by those who, like Job, have come to know their absolute and awful need of God. At this point God is no longer hidden but lives within us."

For Albert Schweitzer God's ways were profoundly hidden. But the hidden God, Schweitzer said at the end of his book, *Quest of the Historical Jesus*, might be understood by reflecting on the Gospel story of Jesus calling the disciples:

> He comes to us as One unknown, without a name, as of old, by the lake side, He came to those . . . who knew Him not. He speaks to us the same word: "Follow thou me!" and sets us to the tasks which He has to fulfill for our time. He commands. And to those who obey Him, whether they be wise or simple, He will reveal Himself in the toils, the conflicts, the sufferings which they shall pass through in His fellowship, and, as an ineffable mystery, they shall learn in their own experience Who He is.

Thanks be to God!

"Sighs Too Deep": Of Lamentation and Hope

Pat Patterson

October 17, 2007

I have a deep sense of sorrow and depression. Our country is, I believe, in a period of profound criminality and loss. It is an era marked by war, murder, and the unleashing of violence in Iraq and Afghanistan; increasing control and exploitation by corporations in the global economy resulting in bourgeoning poverty; denial of devastating assaults on the environment; and erosion of constitutional, civil, and human rights. The escalation of destruction on every side gives me a sense of despair, and I wonder if redemption is possible.

These days I confess that I have difficulty praying. I cannot ask forgiveness, only mercy. The solidarity of sin confronts me at every turn. I feel a sense of responsibility for the state of the world, because I am both a Christian accountable to God for neighbors and for creation, and an American, for whom the nature of democracy, government of the people, is that we cannot divorce ourselves from our leaders and our nation's policies. The words of Romans 8 ring in my heart and reflect both pain and promise.

> We know that the whole creation has been groaning in labor pains until now; and not only the creation, but we ourselves. . . . Likewise the Spirit helps us in our weakness; for we do not know how to pray as we ought, but that very Spirit intercedes with sighs too deep for words. And God, who searches the heart, knows what is the mind of the Spirit, because the Spirit intercedes for the saints according to the will of God. (Romans 8:22-23a, 26-27)

ILLUSION

We Americans have been for too long a people of illusions, confusing our grand vision with the reality of our national life. Analysis of our nation demands application of prophetic and spiritual dimensions, not only political, economic, social, and geopolitical. We have denied the horror of our crimes, including Native American genocide, African American slavery, and military and economic intervention into other lands. We have used and believed propaganda to meld a disparate

11

people into "the American people," while relegating minorities and their history to the periphery and imposing racist patterns on our society and much of the rest of the world. We have permitted the elite power structures to keep us bound to their myths and allowed them to destroy our popular alliances through divide and conquer. We have fomented an aggressive frontier spirit that runs roughshod over peoples and nature, while feigning innocence and self-righteousness. It is an irony of our existence that we have been a generous, idealistic people, whose crimes and shadow side have been denied and repressed. Our own ideals are our most demanding judges.

It is the language of illusion and delusion that has brought us into the war with Iraq. The war on terror has been cast in terms of cosmic struggle between good and evil. No self-criticism tempers the political and military policies that resulted in the brief but ferocious attack on Iraq when it invaded Kuwait in early 1991; the dozen years of embargo that the United Nations estimates resulted in the deaths of half a million Iraqi children; and now the nearly five years of military assault that have killed more than a million people, unleashed sectarian violence, destroyed the infrastructure and historical treasures of that ancient civilization, and ripped apart what was a dictatorial state but nevertheless one of the most advanced countries in the Middle East. In the ravaging of Iraq, there has been little or no attention to proportionality, the tools of diplomacy, and concern for the people. Such savagery goes on under the guise of bringing freedom and democracy. Not even genuine concern for our own troops with their grave physical and psychological wounds has stopped the surge to further destruction.

As James Carroll has written, "Once a war begins, everyone is a war criminal." Or in Rabbi Abraham Heschel's words, "Few are guilty; all are responsible." The idolatry of our illusions blinds us and leads our nation into massacre after massacre and exploitation after exploitation. We watch while Power plays the big game, and we the people play around with our ballots, our political parties, our Congressional lists, our flags and bunting, our slogans praising the "greatest nation on earth."

DISILLUSION

William Sloane Coffin cuts to the quick: "Who gave you the right to be illusioned in the first place?" When we begin seriously examining our history, we see how a sense of superiority, of calling ourselves a city set on a hill, of acting as the last refuge of people seeking freedom, mark our social and religious psyches. Manifest destiny is like a virus in our patriotic bloodstream. The idolatry of privileged patriotism gives our civil religion a particular virulence. Our Christianity, and probably our Judaism, maybe even our Islam, in the American context, run the danger of pollution. The American mythic story is so powerful; it overrides even our altars with its stars and stripes flag. In this American ideological jumble, where is God? When it comes to matters of justice and injustice, of war and peace, where do religion and conscience fit?

Washing over me are moments of coming face to face with the results of evil and questions of my complicity. I stand in the graveyard at Wounded Knee while a descendant of Indian massacres, old and recent, tells the stories of death by guns as well as deprivation and poverty. I ride a train from Kobe to Hiroshima with a man who experienced the atomic bombing and wants to know if Americans really know what it was like and whether it is the kind of thing that a "Christian" nation should do, even in wartime. I sit in the entry to a restaurant in Pyongyang beside an elderly North Korean Christian leader who with anguish still fresh in his soul, asks me why American planes destroyed even the churches where people had gone for refuge believing that they would be safe. I cannot answer but I remember US generals saying that when the Korean War ended, there was nothing left to bomb. I lean against the wall of the tiny museum at My Lai while several elderly women recall the day that American soldiers massacred almost every person in their village.

It is not enough to salve my tender conscience that I contribute to projects related to Native Americans in South Dakota, and that I have worked on changing government and church policies related to Vietnam, North Korea, and now Iraq. The burden remains. Part of it is the fact that death is still being dealt out constantly in my name, and part of it is that I still have too much illusion in my citizen life. But it is also because disillusioned, I am disempowered.

LAMENTATION

For me this is a time of lamentation. The cries of Israel's suffering community in the 6th century B.C.E. provide one insightful starting point for thinking about lamentation. It was a time of loss of national sovereignty. After the fall of Jerusalem in 557 BC, someone in deep agony wrote five poems of lament. As the commentary in the American Bible points out, these songs of tortured sadness express profound grief, sinful responsibility, and enduring hope. These are the cries of victims, now helpless and weak, impoverished and homeless, in the midst of famine, physical destruction, and carnage, comparing their favorable life in the past with this catastrophe. They feel tormented by their enemies and their own people, even by God. They recognize not merely political outcomes but God's judgment on them. The account is drenched in pain, grief, guilt, and betrayal. But it is also full of a sense of collective responsibility and of continuing trust in God.

Usually when we think of lamentations, we think of people who are oppressed, enslaved, victims of terrible crimes against them. The poor, marginalized, exploited and violently repressed cry out in their misery. Their lamentation and aspirations rise to God, a continual incense. But with immense courage, many wait and work for justice in their lives, often searching their hearts and analyzing their societies to see the places where they were complicit in the evil that befell them.

But increasingly I know there is also the lament of the oppressor, who is part of systems that enslave and victimize people. Many of us who are people of conscience and compassion and yet part of this superpower nation, are in a time of heart-wrenching lamentation. We feel betrayed by our own people, leaders lying and leading us into a cruel, illegal, unjust war against the people of Afghanistan and Iraq. We imagine the mangled and dying and the tremendous grief of people mourning the loss of their dear ones in war. We are horrified by the use of torture and the defense of its use. We are angered to see national wealth going to pay for war and to benefit corporations that are already reaping tremendous profit. We are dishonored by the dismissing of international treaties and international law. We grieve at the destruction and despoliation of earth, sea, and sky. We fear for the future of the earth and all its inhabitants.

We grieve at the decline of health care, education, and other community services. We observe the growth of military and police security and the neglect of what makes healthy and thriving communities. We recognize the shrinking of democracy with the influence of big money in our elections, the impact of the Patriot Act, decreasing government accountability, increasing citizen disillusionment and apathy, and growing racism, poverty, and discrimination in our society. Our priorities as a country have been turned upside down, so that what is promoted and protected is not the people's welfare. It is rather the welfare of the corporations, military interests, and political elites. Wealth has become god, whether as exploitative greed or as consumerism. Our illusions have come face to face with the dangerous forces of contemporary politics and war. Our false "heavenly kingdom," made up of republic, democracy, and Bill of Rights, is collapsing at our feet, even as it keeps on shattering the lives of millions of people at home and abroad.

We recognize that we, too, like those 2500 years ago, know the meaning of the destruction of the temple and the desecration of our religious beliefs, not so much by external but internal forces. We see that our rituals and worship are often twisted and corrupted. Our relationship with God is sabotaged by our guilt, neglect of justice and failure to work fully for what makes for peace. We are appalled at the blessing of war; we are shocked at the privileging of the wealthy and powerful. But too often we wonder if we are too nice and meek and depressed to carry on the struggle that needs to be done. We too quietly tolerate the distortions of our faith, outside and inside ourselves. We feel like exiles in our own land. We have few brave and bold voices to counter corrupt, greedy, and militaristic leaders. Sometimes we feel as if we have been overpowered by a coup of the neocon/theocons, as Joseph Wilson calls them.

As Christians in a country at war we have a sense of treason against God. How can we pay for and support the killing of people in Iraq, and withhold resources from the starving and struggling at home and around the world? Is this not sin against the Holy Spirit, the holy that dwells in each person? How can we face the compassionate and merciful God who loves all the people of the world? Is not our country under severe judgment? We join Jesus in his lament as he wept over the city of Jerusalem, "If you, even you, had recognized on this day the things that make for peace!" (Luke 19:42) And we know we are the ones he weeps over today.

HOPE

But can it be that sorrow and lamentation open a road to responsibility and redemptive action? The biblical ancients seem always to have paired their cries of pain with recognition of the need for repentance. Owning responsibility, whether as victim or victimizer, sets the stage for reaffirming God's steadfast love and listening to the call to rebuild in the midst of the ruins and make change for a future not bound by the past

There is catharsis in lamentation, for it wakens us to reality, forces us to compare the illusion with reality, brings us back to confession and repentance, restores compassion for the broken, and invites us to walk faithfully in the ways of justice and peace. It breaks our idols and false images. Our grief and tears are tools for conversion. Creating a new heart within us becomes the call to create a new world around us. The God who leads us forth out of despair and disillusion is steadfast love and courageous possibility. This is the One who has given us rebirth and resurrection.

Our involvement in struggle for change is a way to draw on God's forgiveness and power. Out of the experience of grief and exile from our true selves may come the consciousness that leads to healing and empowerment. Recognizing our complicity as victimizers, deeply mired in pain and guilt, we can make new beginnings and gain strength for reform and revolution. Lament as analysis of the present reality and our role in it, and lamentation as truth-telling, are a launching pad for a new world. Lamentation and repentance are twin engines for change. We stand in the gap between what is and what ought to be, weeping and hoping, distraught and trustful.

Grounded in a realistic understanding of the power of death and the demonic, we know that we cannot underestimate evil. We are aware of how the good can be turned to the bad and the ideal to the destructive. Uncovering our idolatries, revealing our lies and crimes, unmasking the forces that pose as saviors but are really dominators and destroyers, these challenges rise up from the heart of our lamentation. And there is significant liberation in personal and communal confession, dynamic power in relationship and responsible community. The cross and the history of other brave struggles of resistance keep us discontent with where we are and remind us that even in the depths, other alternatives are awaiting our commitment. The foundation is a loving and just God in a universe of possibility, novelty, and freedom.

Rosemary Radford Ruether, in her book *America, Amerikka: Elect Nation and Imperial Violence*, proposes for the oppressor a "theology of letting go" as the counterpoint to liberation theology for the oppressed. She describes in brief the agenda: "Such a theology of liberation and letting go must involve, not only a transformed relationship between rich and poor in the United States and between the United States and the rest of the world, but also the relation of the rich and poor to the earth itself, to the eco-community of our common planetary home." Dr. Ruether states even more urgently the priority issues for us Americans: "extreme economic disparities worldwide, environmental destruction and inflated American military power." (250-

51, 266) This challenge is to all of us who despair and hope.

We need to let go of illusion and disillusion; we need to let our lamentation lead us to hope. And if we would hope, we would follow Jesus. A man of lamentation, he understood the gap between the brutal Roman occupation and the reign of God. He confronted the dehumanization and disempowerment of the people. Standing in the powerful God-history of his people and the prophets, he would not give up the tradition of liberation. In table fellowship he gathered the despairing and guilty, those impoverished by Empire and those profiting from it. He healed and cared, overcoming social isolation and demon possession. He gave alternatives: love the enemy, trust like flowers and birds, care for one another, set priorities that put God and neighbor first, find the ways of peace, share wealth and justice. He guided us toward letting go.

In the midst of the worst conditions, Jesus leads us to seize the new day, make the fresh start, create leavening models on a small scale like salt and light. He didn't exactly tell us what to do, but he made us think about what to do. He showed us that as we seek first the reign of God, all the other parts of our lives and our visions will take their rightful place.

In the end we know that his compassionate and visionary way will not take away our tears over the suffering people of the world or wipe out our disappointment and guilt over the failures and misbegotten policies of our government. As long as power is abused and people die needlessly, as long as we are complicit in and profit from our powerful nation, we will not know rest and relief. We must denounce what is destructive and announce what is just and beneficial. Judgment marches beside us. We cannot be silent or inactive. We must repent, resist, re-vision. Our call is to join God in renewing the earth. When we let go of the power of privilege and domination, we will gain the power to transform our nation and world. With confession and compassion, courage and caring, we have critical work to do.

In the end, I believe that the Spirit does intercede with sighs too deep for words. And I believe that Jesus does take us through lamentation to hope. And I believe that the steadfast love of God accompanies us down all the paths of this time and place, our critical moment in history.

My Search for Jesus
Jean W. Underwood
November 14, 2007

The Song of a Heathen
(Sojourning in Galilee, A. D. 32)
Richard Watson Gilder

I

If Jesus Christ is a man, —
And only a man, — I say
That of all mankind I cleave to him,
And to him will I cleave always.

II

If Jesus Christ is a God, —
And the only God, — I swear
I will follow Him through heaven and hell,
The earth, the sea, and the air!

I knew he was God. I had discovered it myself at the age of thirteen
when I first read through the Bible as a new Christian. (Friends had
warned me to begin with the New Testament and to skip the "begats.") I
fell in love with the Jesus I met in Matthew, Mark, and Luke. Then I
came to John. What in the world was he talking about? The Word?
What was that? I finally gave up on the first five verses and pushed on.
Then I came to verse 14, "The Word was made flesh and dwelt among
us." They were talking about Jesus! Goose pimples. Hair on end.
Jesus was God! Subsequent Christian teaching refined that idea.
Seminary training honed it.

I read more of John. I did not like the Jesus John wrote about.
All of those pompous-sounding, "I ams"!

Through the years I came to love the Gospel of John. The "I
ams" became precious as I experienced them in my Christian life. "I am
the way, the truth, and the life. No one comes to the Father but by me."
(14:6) I wonder. Would I have become a missionary if I had not
believed that? Probably not.

All of that changed in August of 2001. I had gone to a

monastery on a mountain above Santa Barbara. I picked up a book in the library to read between meetings. It was on mysticism. To my great surprise not all of the authors were Christian. They came from many different religions. With no knowledge (?) or thought of Jesus they had come to God. They had experienced God in ways that I had thought only Christians could! I was amazed. I was also thrilled by the grace of God revealed in their writings.

The next morning I went outside to my favorite bench which overlooks the ocean to have my usual quiet time. There was a thick fog. I was praising God when "it" happened. "It" was a mystical experience of the Oneness of all things. All is One. All is God. There is nothing that is not God, yet God is infinitely, unimaginably MORE than all things. I felt as if I were being absorbed into the fog, into God. It was Heaven. It was ecstasy, sheer ecstasy!

This experience, and the reading I had done leading up to it, turned my world upside down. It set me on two quests. The first quest was to find out what had happened to me (see Vol. I of this *Doing Theology* series). The need for a second quest emerged slowly. I first noticed that I could no longer recite the Apostles' Creed. Then one of my favorite hymns was lost to me, "Holy, holy, holy, . . . blessed Trinity." Trinity? All is One! By Christmas of 2001 I had to acknowledge that what I had believed about Jesus was no longer tenable. I never doubted the incarnation, but if *all* is One then the *logos* incarnate in Jesus is none other than the Holy Spirit who indwells us. Was Jesus just like us after all? What could I now believe? I needed to find out. This is the story of my second quest.

Source Materials
Our information about Jesus comes primarily from the Bible. Contemporary Christian opinion about the Bible varies all of the way from "it's true" to "it's false." (Take the simplest meaning, as in a true-false test.) In seminary I had gained an educated balance between the two extremes. Then for forty years I worked with Korean Christians who took it to be "true." My quest led me in the opposite direction, to the Jesus Seminar, whose premise seems to be, "False, unless proven true" (see below). Last I turned to the early Christian writings that did not get into the Bible.

1. The Gospels
I turned first to the Gospels, reading them with new eyes, but no

insight came. This was not surprising as I had been reading and studying them for decades. Edersheim (*Life and Times of Jesus the Messiah*, 1906) was always at hand, as was my husband John, a seminary Bible professor.

Help did come from my continued reading of the Old Testament. In Jeremiah 1:5 I came upon these words, "Before I formed you in the womb I knew you, and before you were born I consecrated you; I appointed you a prophet to the nations." If this was true of the prophet Jeremiah, it was certainly true of God's Messiah. Jesus had been created for a very special purpose indeed.

I reread Reynolds Price's imaginative *Three Gospels* (Mark, John, and Price)

I borrowed a copy of the Gospel of Thomas. I found it hard to read. It is just a bunch of disconnected sayings. Many of them were familiar. Some of them made no sense at all. I needed a teacher! I began to really empathize with those who find the Bible difficult to read, and understand why Jesus' disciples were constantly asking him to explain his sayings.

2. The Jesus Seminar

The Jesus Seminar is a group of New Testament scholars who meet together to read papers and discuss them. They received a great deal of media attention around the time of the publication of their *Five Gospels* in 1993 (Matthew, Mark, Luke, John, and Thomas). The "Five Gospels" are color-coded. The colors were decided by vote. The voting was open to the public, and was done by color-coded beads:

> *Red:*   *That's Jesus!*
> *Pink:*   *Sure sounds like Jesus.*
> *Gray:*   *Well, maybe.*
> *Black: There's been some mistake.*

Two members of the Seminar and a critic of it have influenced my thinking.

James Robinson is a fellow Pilgrim Place resident and friend. I have heard him speak several times and read some of his books. I am most grateful to Jim, however, for his work in making the Nag Hammadi codices accessible to scholars everywhere.

The works of **Marcus Borg** are well known here at Pilgrim Place. Early in my quest someone suggested that I read *Meeting Jesus*

Again for the First Time. I did, and was captivated. I particularly liked his portrayal of Jesus as a "spirit person," a "mediator of the sacred," "one of those persons in human history to whom the Spirit was an experiential reality." Borg then mentions several others whom he also considers to be "spirit" people (32). I went on to read more. *The God We Never Knew* has been most helpful, particularly the section on *Jesus and God.* Borg writes of the "pre-Easter Jesus" and the "post-Easter Jesus." I realized that the one I was searching for was the pre-Easter Jesus, but he can only be found in post-Easter writings.

Suppose those of us in this room were to write an article on the Civil Rights movement of America in the 60s. Those of you who were involved in the movement at that time will have vivid memories. Those who have continued to teach and preach about civil rights, studying, conferring, rethinking and organizing materials, will have a wide range of knowledge and experience to pass on. Yet we would all be writing with post-60s vision and understanding. How true a picture of the actual events could we still pass on? We would also all be writing with "bias ." There is not a person among us who thinks that segregation was a good thing and should have been continued. Even so, I think I would color the best of our reports *red-pink.*

In February of 2005 I joined a Lenten discussion group who were reading *Meeting Jesus Again for the First Time.* The leader, Dick Johnson, a local historian, suggested that we also look at **Luke Timothy Johnson**'s *The Real Jesus.* This book is a critique of the Seminar and its methodology.

Johnson discusses a number of the criteria used by historians to determine whether the material at hand is factual or not. Among these is the method "of locating converging lines of evidence   When ten witnesses disagree vehemently on whether the noise that they heard at midnight was a car backfire, a gunshot, or a firecracker, it becomes highly probable that a loud percussive sound occurred about that time." (112)

A number of the Gospel narratives fall into this category. When the Gospel writings agree too closely, it is supposed that Matthew and Luke copied from Mark, or from the yet-to-be-discovered *source,* "Q." (Robinson has published a hypothetical reconstruction of Q.)

There is very little which is considered to be reliable *historical* data about Jesus. Most of what we have comes through the Church, a biased source. The source materials for Socrates are considered better. Among other things, his enemies also wrote of him.

3. The Apocrypha

Wilhelm Schneemelcher in his introduction to the Sixth edition (German) of *The New Testament Apocrypha* explains the included documents as, "writings which have not been received into the canon, but which by title and other statements lay claim to be in the same class with the writings of the canon." He goes on to say that some of these Gospels were "intended to take the place of the four Gospels of the canon . . . or to stand as an enlargement of them side by side with them." Other materials are also included "on the ground that older traditions live on in them." Translations from the Nag Hammadi codices appear in the later editions.

The New Testament Apocrypha is a daunting work. I have read only Volume I, the part concerning the Gospels. In the end I read it as I had been reading the Bible: a little from the Old Testament and a little from the New, day by day, as part of my quiet time. It took me more than a year.

An early conclusion was that the makers of the canon had done a good job. Nothing in the Apocrypha can even compare with the canonical Gospels. Even so, here and there I found interesting material which has added to my understanding of the scriptures. Here are a few of my findings:

"In the Gospel of the Nazareans the reason is given why John was known to the high priest. As he was the son of the poor fisherman Zebedee, he had often brought fish to the palace of the high priests Annas and Caiaphas. And John went out to the damsel that kept the door and secured from her permission for his companion Peter, who stood weeping loudly before the door, to come in." (164)

The New Testament barely mentions two events which have long puzzled me. One is the "descent into hell/Hades" of the Apostles' Creed, and the other is about the dead who were raised with Jesus. Matthew reports that when Jesus died, ". . . tombs also were opened, and many bodies of the saints who had fallen asleep were raised, and coming out of the tombs after his resurrection they went into the holy city and appeared to many." (Mt 27:52-53) 1 Peter 3:18-19 speaks of Jesus "being put to death in the flesh but made alive in the spirit; in which he went and preached to the spirits in prison . . ." The Apocrypha has entire books devoted to these subjects. Names are given, stories are told, and supposed conversations are invented. These teachings must have been of great importance to early Christians for them to have been described in such detail.

In sheer volume of material, after Jesus, James the Just, the "brother of the Lord," gets the most attention. Thomas comes second. Peter, of course, figures prominently. Paul is barely mentioned. More is devoted to Mary Magdalene. Does this indicate what was considered important to the early church (certainly James was!), or is it merely an accident of document preservation and the location in which the fragments happen to have been found? (Thomas seems to have been very important to the church in Syria.)

A number of the Apocryphal materials seem to have been written to fill in the gaps. Whole gospels were written about Jesus' childhood. There is an account of Mary's life and family (*The Protevangelium of James*). Stories are told of Joseph of Arimathea in hiding after the resurrection. Many of the materials are from Gnostic sources. Some of these purport to be the teachings of Jesus during the forty days between the resurrection and the ascension.

I return to the Apocrypha from time to time. I read the story of Mary during Advent and the *Gospel of Peter* at Easter. I like the *Gospel of the Nazareans* very much, and puzzling parts of the sayings in the *Coptic Gospel of Thomas* are beginning to make more sense. If I were to color-code the Apocrypha, the *Nazareans* and more than half of *Thomas* would be *pink-red;* most of the rest would be *black-gray*. There are exceptions, of course. The martyrdom of James, by being cast down from the pinnacle of the Temple, seems to be accepted by all, but some of the accounts of what happened next are strange indeed!

My pre-Easter Jesus

I mentally color-code the synoptic Gospels basically *red-pink*. Like our hypothetical accounts of the 60s, they were written some thirty to forty years after the events. Eyewitnesses were still around. Memories could be shared and corrected. I also believe that the Holy Spirit had a part in the whole process.

John is definitely a post-Easter work. Even among the early Church Fathers there was doubt as to its factual accuracy. Yet there are many things about the life of Jesus, generally accepted as true, which we know only because John wrote of them.

This is how I imagine Jesus' life to have been during the years of his public ministry.

He began by preaching, "Repent, for the kingdom of heaven is at hand," the same message that John the Baptist had proclaimed (Mt. 4:17 and 3:2). He taught in the synagogues and began to gather disciples.

23

Mark gives us a picture of what may have been a typical Sabbath (Ch. 2). It took place in Capernaum near the beginning of Jesus' ministry. They went to the synagogue in the morning and Jesus taught. He also cast out a demon. They went to Peter's house for lunch, but found Peter's mother-in-law sick in bed with a fever. Jesus healed her and she got up and ministered to them. In the evening, when the Sabbath had ended and people were free to move about, "they brought to him all who were sick or possessed with demons. And the whole city was gathered together at the door." The crowds. Always the crowds!

Jesus needed to get alone to pray. In the dark of night, while the others were sleeping, he slipped out of the city to a "lonely place." They woke in the morning to find him gone and began a search. When his friends finally did find him, they complained, "Everyone is searching for you." But Jesus only said, "Let us go on to the next towns, that I may preach there also; for that is why I came out." And so the itineration began.

Jesus was accompanied not only by his disciples, but also by a small group of women who did what they could to help (Lk. 8:1-3). On occasion Jesus set off for lonely places with just the disciples, but they could not remain hidden for long. He continued to seek time apart to pray. He attended most of the religious festivals in Jerusalem, once passing through Samaria to do so.

Jesus' growing popularity soon attracted the attention of the religious authorities and they began to hound him even as they had hounded John the Baptist, hoping to catch him in something they could use to discredit him. John had called them "vipers." Jesus called them "hypocrites, blind fools, and blind guides" (Mt. 23).

I have found no record anywhere to indicate that Jesus ever criticized the Roman authorities. He commended the Roman centurion for his faith. He counseled the paying of taxes and paid them himself. In the Sermon on the Mount he had the audacity to suggest that if you were compelled (by a Roman soldier) to go one mile you should go two! (Law allowed the Roman soldiers to demand one.)

I think of Jesus primarily as a teacher. He taught not only in the synagogues but wherever and whenever he could make the opportunity to do so. He once got into a boat to distance himself from the crowd so as to be able to sit and teach them.

Jesus was a man of his culture. Borg points out that he used "the classic forms of wisdom speech (parables . . . aphorisms)" (*Meeting Jesus*, 30), but Jesus turned everything upside down. I grew up learning the meaning of the parables even as I heard the story—thinking, "Why couldn't they figure that out?" Once when I was reading through the Gospel of Thomas, a passage that had previously puzzled me suddenly jumped out full of meaning. There was nothing new or startling in the message, but I was amazed and delighted at the way Jesus had put it. He was a captivating teacher.

With some thirty years of Jesus' life to report on, the canonical Gospel writers devote from one quarter to one third of their material to just one week, the week from Palm Sunday to Easter. It began on a **Sunday** morning with his provocative entry into Jerusalem, riding on a donkey, thus fulfilling the scripture to suggest that he was the Messiah, coming in peace. Jesus then proceeded to the Temple where he cast out the moneychangers and those who were doing business there. (Mark says he just looked around. It was the next day when he cast them out.)

Jesus spent **Monday** and **Tuesday** teaching in the Temple. His enemies joined the crowd around him. They asked seemingly innocent questions, hoping to entrap him. They had already determined to kill him, but secretly, not during the festival for fear of a riot. Judas played into their hands.

Wednesday. Judas was busy, setting up the betrayal. Jesus may have been busy too, searching out a place where he could eat the last supper with his disciples. (There is nothing in writing about this.)

On **Thursday** Jesus sent Peter and John into the city to make preparations for the "Passover" meal. He didn't tell them where to go but said instead, "As you go into the city a man carrying a jar of water will meet you." (What? A man carrying water? That's women's work! He should be easy to spot.) "Follow him." That evening none of the other disciples knew where they were going as they traveled together. This meal was not to be interrupted! According to John, Judas did not stay to the end of the meal but was sent out early. Judas did know about the garden of Gethsemane.

Friday. The cross. John places the sacrificing of the Passover lamb in the Temple at the very time Jesus was on the cross. (Edersheim has a long explanation for the discrepancy in the timing of the Passover meal as reported by the synoptics and John.) For the people of Jesus' time, accustomed as they were to the idea of the necessity of animal sacrifices for the atonement of sin, the entire story of the Passion is of tremendous significance. It is well known. I will pass on.

Saturday. The grave. And, the "descent into hell (Hades)." (I color this *gray*. See above.)

Sunday. Easter. The empty tomb!

The post-Easter Jesus

They were slow to believe. It was too-good-to-be-true! But gradually the women, and then the disciples, became convinced that Jesus had indeed risen bodily from the grave.

The resurrection body was different. Jesus appeared in a closed room. They sometimes failed to recognize him. Yet he ate and could be handled. Once he even cooked breakfast for them. For some "forty" days they expected to see him any place and any time. Some time before Pentecost he was "taken up," taken into God.

Where am I now?

Theologically I am very much drawn to Borg's description of Jesus as a "spirit person." At this point I can't improve on that.

In my imagination I ponder on what it would have been like to have been there then, to have walked with Jesus, to have sat and listened to him teach. I plan to go to the Holy Land this spring with the group from Pilgrim Place. I'm hoping that the trip will enlarge my understanding of many things, including the life of Jesus.

June 2008

I've been there now, to that troubled, war-torn land. On the surface here and there are beautiful thriving cities. Digging down, way down, here and there are sites commemorating events in the life of Jesus. I've seen enough now to have a feel for what it might have been like then.

The incarnation and the resurrection remain a mystery. Once there lived a Man who taught us the way of peace. Is anyone willing to listen?

Gifts from the Parish

Peter A. O'Reilly

November 28, 2007

A: The heavens declare the glory of God (Psalm 19: 1)

The winter of 1941 was a cold and difficult one as were all the winters of my childhood years. I had just turned seven, and the short days and long nights were especially hard to bear. The war was at its height and, though it was far away and little understood by me, the fact that there was no candy in the local shops, not even a bar of chocolate, was a matter of great disappointment and deep concern. But Christmas was on its way and Mom had said that Santa, who had never failed me before, would surely find sweets somewhere. My eldest brother Terence, always the pessimist, had his doubts. There was nothing for me to do but wait and hope.

Finally, Christmas Day arrived. I had slept fitfully the night before and several times thought that I had heard Santa coming down the chimney with his bag of toys and, hope against hope, a plentiful supply of candy. At a very early hour, still fast asleep, my mother woke me up and told me the good news. Santa had indeed come but I was not to open the presents until we had returned from church. It was not easy for her to get all nine of us kids ready and on time, since Dad had died just four years before; but somehow she managed to get us all out the door for the journey to the early morning Mass. I wondered what the others had got from Santa and asked my youngest sister Carmel what presents she got, as we stepped out into the dark and numbing cold. She mumbled something that was lost in the bitter wind that blew from the north. I reached for the gloved and reassuring hand of my mother and we set off down the narrow road toward the village church a little over a mile away.

The sky was cloudless and the stars shone bright and very clear in the winter darkness. The sun would not rise for at least another hour and the sliver of a moon in the western sky was of little help. All over the countryside scattered houses had lighted candles in their windows, a sign of welcome to Mary and Joseph should they need a place to stay. We passed by the home of James and Mary Wilson. There were no candles in the windows. The house seemed so dark and very lonely. I wondered aloud why they had no sign of Christmas and suggested to Mom that people who had no children did not put lighted candles in their windows. She said nothing but held my hand a little tighter, no doubt privy to the pain of the childless couple.

We continued on our way, our shoes cracking the ice that had formed in the puddles of water during the nighttime cold. The voices of unseen neighbors began to break the morning silence as they too made their way to the early morning Mass. Somewhere in the distance a barking dog voiced his annoyance to the morning sky and then was silent. His sleep had probably been disturbed by other people also on their way to church.

In a short while we reached the village, and neighbors whose voices I recognized appeared as if by magic through the enveloping darkness. There were no streetlights to help us on our way, but we all knew the narrow laneway well. In a short while we were at the church door and made our way up the aisle that was dimly lit by feeble candles placed a few paces apart.

"Can I go to see if Jesus has come?" I asked my mother. "We will have to wait until Father Higgins blesses the crèche and then all will be ready," she whispered. The church was filling up fast and I found it difficult to know any of the people towering above me. The few candles scattered around the church only made the darkness more intense. I stayed close to my mother and siblings.

Then Miss Kelly, our first grade teacher, called her small choir to order and started to play as the priest and servers entered the church. "O come, all ye faithful," they sang, their thin, earnest voices almost drowned by Miss Kelly's aggressive thumping on the ancient, asthmatic harmonium. When Mass was over, I hurried to the crib. Yes, Jesus was there surrounded by animals and some richly-clad figures coming in from the right. Joseph stood somewhat self-consciously in the background as Mary knelt by the straw-lined bed of her newborn son. Then we all hurried home to breakfast and the opening of gifts. Santa had brought me a prized bar of chocolate, two pieces of candy and a small wooden puzzle. The dinner of turkey-with-stuffing, roasted potatoes, plenty of gravy to be followed by plum pudding, sent by a thoughtful cousin living in New York, filled out a very event-filled day.

It was a magical time that Christmas of 1941.[1] It began for me

---

[1] Mircea Eliade, in *The Sacred and the Profane*, writes of "some parts of space (being) qualitatively different from others" as when "the Lord says to Moses, take off your shoes for the place where you stand is holy ground." Both time and space were "sacred" that Christmas of 1941, different from all the rest of the year. Rudolf Otto, in *The Idea of the Holy*, writes of the "*mysterium tremendum*, the

in darkness and the arrival of Santa, and the walk to Mass between frost-covered fields and the little church packed with family and neighbors and the smell of incense. Even the stars and welcoming windows of the widely-scattered farmhouses spoke of a "presence" that filled me with a wonder I could not articulate and did not need to. That night I went to bed tired but happy, and said my prayers to a God I knew for certain watched over me and all my family. Then I slept.

It was probably in the wonder of that Christmas morning that I first became a "theologian"!

B: What has Athens to do with Jerusalem? (Tertullian)

I had gone to the seminary in the mid 1950s, when it was the accepted wisdom that one should be dubious of what the world outside had to offer. In fact, we were led to believe that the less we had to do with the world outside the better. Our role was to be that of teacher rather than pupil, preacher rather than listener. One could well describe this approach as an excess of smugness mingled with arrogance, but we did have precedent on our side. About the year 200, an articulate and recent convert from North Africa had come to the same conclusion. He did not believe that the Church had any need of help from the larger world of Greek philosophy and learning. "What has Athens to do with Jerusalem?"[1] he asked rhetorically. His answer was clear, dismissive and confident: in a word, nothing. His name was Quintus Septimus Florens Tertullianus, (c.160-220), Tertullian for short. By and large we shared his prejudice and his self-assurance. That confidence, however, was soon to be shaken.

Just eighteen months before I was ordained, Pope John XXIII announced his plan to convoke the Church's twenty-first Ecumenical Council, the first since Vatican I of 1869-70. At first, the news had little impact upon my fellow seminarians or me. We looked up our history

---

truly 'mysterious' object which is beyond our apprehension and comprehension, not only because our knowledge has certain irremovable limits, but because in it we come upon something inherently 'wholly other,' whose kind and character are incommensurable with our own, and before which we therefore recoil in a wonder that strikes us chill and numb." (28)

[1] Tertullian (c. 160-220): "What indeed has Athens to do with Jerusalem? (*Quid Athenae Hierosolymis?*) . . . What concord is there between the Academy and the Church? What between heretics and Christians? Our instruction comes from the porch of Solomon . . . Away with all attempts to produce a mottled Christianity of Stoic, Platonic and dialectic composition!" (*De Praescriptione*, VII).

books and read of the other twenty or so councils and the myriad local assemblies dating back as far as the Council of Jerusalem in Acts 15. The preparation for the opening of the Council went on apace, but we were all too busy or disinterested to pay much attention.

When the first session of the Council began on October 11 of 1962, tantalizing reports of new ways of being Church began to filter through the news media. The Church I had grown up in was clearly receiving a thorough airing out. The disclosures of the often-heated discussions and of the documents being drawn up by the bishops and theologians read at times like spy stories when published in the *New Yorker* magazine. The source of the leaks was a mysterious writer named Xavier Rynne. He was something like "Deep Throat," Bob Woodward and Carl Bernstein all rolled into one! His reports from Rome made for exciting reading, all the more because they were clandestine.

I began to read the news each day with mounting excitement. The document that really caught my attention, and the attention of most of the world it seemed, was published on December 7, 1965. Its opening words, *Gaudium et Spes* (joy and hope) said it all. The world was God's creation, all of it, and was to be embraced with joy, not kept at arm's length. It invited all believers to enter into dialogue with the larger world, for, "The joys and the hopes, the griefs and the anxieties of the men [*sic*] of this age . . . these too are the joys and hopes, the griefs and anxieties of the followers of Christ."[1] The world was no longer to be shunned but embraced, not ignored but engaged in dialogue.

It was all such heady stuff for me. After five years of parish life I had begun to feel uneasy. I needed to move beyond the God whom I found in the wonder and awe of that long-ago Christmas morning, and I definitely needed a change of diet from the largely ossified theology I was fed in my seminary classes.

Around that time, I had begun to recover an interest I once had in English literature. A classmate who was going on to further studies said to me, "People today do not read theological text books. Whatever 'theology' they have comes from their own struggles with life, the novels they read and especially the films they see. You should go back to pursuing your studies in English." That was the encouragement I needed. I realized with mounting excitement that the world of literature

---

[1] Preface to Pastoral Constitution on the *Church in the Modern World*.

had as much to say to me then, perhaps even more, as it had when I was in high school and later on in college.

I remembered especially how fascinated I was when we studied the character of Satan in Milton's *Paradise Lost*, to give an example. Here was someone I could appreciate, who refused to bow to convention, even to his creator. Although utterly defeated, he was still unbowed. That appealed to my then-defiant teen-age years: What though the field be lost.[1] This was the 60s and I felt even more rebellious and in need of change than I did during my younger days. More than anything else, I wanted to have a better understanding of what was happening in that rapidly-changing era of the Beatles, Berkeley and Woodstock.

I was hopeful that I would find ways of access into the minds of believers and nonbelievers alike (and, I should mention, into myself as well), through a study of the plays, novels and films that spoke to their lives and described their experiences. I applied for the Master's program in English Literature in Loyola University, Los Angeles, and was accepted.

My first course there was God in Modern Literature. The teacher was a Jesuit whose range of interests encompassed not only the world of literature but also the worlds of music, film, art and architecture. Each of these fields of human endeavor, he told us many times, would help us to understand a little better the ceaseless search of humanity for the God who is beyond all human expression. At school that first semester, literature became for me the gateway into a world about which I knew little but needed to know much more. How much more I needed to know I was soon to find out.

At that time, I was assigned to Good Shepherd parish, in Beverly Hills. On August 9, 1967, I had gone to visit one of the parishioners and on my way home I heard over the radio that there had been a murder just north of Sunset Boulevard. Even though the crime had been committed close to where I lived, I paid little attention. I had many other things to do that day.

Just as I walked in the door of the house where I lived, the phone was ringing. A policeman told me that there had been a homicide, gave me an address and asked me to come as soon as possible. So this was

---

[1] John Milton, *Paradise Lost*, Bk 1, 105-111: "What though the field be lost? / All is not lost; the unconquerable will / And study of revenge, immortal hate, / And courage never to submit or yield: / And what is else not to be overcome? / That glory never shall his wrath or might / Extort from me."

what the news item was about, I thought. My heart began to beat faster. When I arrived at the house, I was taken aback when a news reporter I knew among the many at the scene told me that there might be up to five victims in all. After I had finished my visit to the gruesome scene, I left shaken and confused. The next few days were a nightmare of calls for information that I either did not have or could not divulge.

Privately, I was very worried as to what I would say when I met with the man whose wife and unborn child, along with four friends, had been so brutally murdered. He had lost his mother in the Holocaust and was not a believer. I searched for a bridge to his world, a world very different from mine. I knew that the usual presumptions of a shared world-view would not work for either of us. Would anything I had to say be even remotely coherent? How would I frame my remarks so as to make some sense to him?

One of the books we had discussed, during my first semester, was *The Plague*, by Albert Camus.[1] In the book, a Dr. Rieux, who was a professed atheist, was caring for the victims of a plague in Oran, Algeria, along with a Fr. Paneloux. Despite their different points of view, and the deep theological divide between them, both worked in the same hospital, helping the victims of the plague. The grieving husband/father and I could also work together just as Rieux and Paneloux did. The summons of Vatican II to engage the world in all its complexity and brokenness, despite very different convictions, seemed to fit our situation precisely. Ironically, it seemed to me, theology might keep us apart, but evil would bring us together.

Most in attendance at the funeral, I took for granted, would have little awareness of Christian beliefs or share anything of the hope in the afterlife. In my seminary training, I was given to understand that all that was necessary on such occasions was to give the message of Jesus in all its unvarnished truth and splendor; it was not necessary to make concessions.

And yet, Jesus did make accommodations for the life experiences of his listeners, through his use of parables and stories. A highhanded confidence in the probative power of the Christian message was really not appropriate on this occasion. I was all the more convinced of the

---

[1] Albert Camus, *The Plague*: Dr. Rieux to Fr. Paneloux: "That child, anyhow, was innocent, father, and you know it as well as I do . . . I shall refuse to love a scheme of things in which children are put to torture . . . We're working side by side for something that unites us and it's the only thing that matters." (New York: Random House, Modern Library, 1948, 196.)

need to build bridges when I read that, in 1946, Camus, for all his overt atheism, had met with a group of Dominican priests and put to them the question: "We are confronted with an evil whose origin we do not know and whose solution we cannot find. If you cannot give us an answer, who else in the world can?"[1] The answer he was given, though it did not satisfy him, was that all, believer and unbeliever alike, should strive to make the world a better place by working together to bring about the good, but that evil on the scale occasioned by World War II was a mystery that only faith could answer.

If a group of French Dominican priests could not give a convincing answer to Camus, what chance would I have at the funeral of answering all the mourners' questions? I did know, however, that many who would attend the service were very influential, indeed powerful, and I should try to harness their concern in the cause of peace and justice. There, at least, I had a starting point and a framework within which to address the dreadful deeds of the past few days. At the funeral, I preached a message of comfort and hope and asked for help in making the world a safer and more loving place. I left the rest to God who, I reminded myself, is not limited by the limitations of his servants. The response I received afterward gave me reason to believe that I was on the right track.

My studies in literature had helped me greatly to understand a world beyond what I had known and to develop a strategy of outreach to "other sheep that do not belong to this fold" (Jn 10: 16). No matter what Tertullian had to say, I realized that believer and nonbelieiver really needed to work together and that Athens and Jerusalem did indeed have much to learn from each other.

C: I believe so that I may understand (St. Anselm)

In 1984, I received a call from the bishop: "I would like you to become pastor at Nativity parish, in El Monte." I had only a vague notion where the parish was and was not too happy about taking on my first parish as pastor in an area about which I knew so little. I had just spent some time in Mexico learning Spanish and thought that this might be as good a place as any for me try out what I had learned. With fear

---

[1] "He (Camus) compared himself with the young Augustine. Evil tormented him and he could not understand why the Church seemed to explain it away . . . Most of the Dominicans were sympathetic because they detected in Camus that need to believe which was, in their eyes but not in his, the starting point of faith." Patrick McCarthy, *Camus* (New York: Random Books, 219.)

and some misgivings, I agreed to accept the assignment.

My first impressions were not too encouraging. The Spanish the people spoke was quite different from the more book-based language I had learned. The pace of life, too, was not what I had become used to. In the years that followed Vatican II, I had attended many of the courses and workshops that were offered to laity and clergy alike. I was excited by the new insights I had gained and was full of plans for implementing them, now that I was pastor. But the enthusiasm I had was not shared by the people. I felt quite defeated and downcast.

I called up a friend one day and asked if I could visit him. He had worked in Hispanic areas for many years. He listened to me without interruption. When I had finished, he said to me, "You are filled with good ideas and plans. The trouble is that you are fixated on doing, on action. The Hispanic people work best when they have a relationship with you first. When they get to know you, they will be much more likely to work with you."

The word "relationship" jumped out at me. It brought me back to what I had read years before, in the writings of St. Anselm (1033-1109). For the likes of St. Anselm, theology was above all relational, not what it later became, a study of the nature of God. "Their (Anselm, Cyprian, Irenaeus, Origen) theology, in the ancient sense of the word, was a hymn, a prayer, the point where knowledge and love become praise (it was a) prayed theology prompted by a devotion to Christ."[1] With this insight from St. Anselm, I would have to start with the building up of relationships with the people, that is, before I could work on programs.

The process of building relationships with people had obvious drawbacks. It was time-consuming and demanded a lot of personal attention. I had become used to a more goal-oriented approach in the largely Anglo parishes where I had been, and I missed the clarity of precise goal-setting and the satisfaction of measurable results. But the building of personal relationships had more lasting effects. The groups we formed bonded better and stayed united longer after the goals had been achieved. Starting anew was always easier because of this.

Best of all for me was the stress the people placed upon prayer. Prayers were very important to them. They were offered at the beginning of each gathering and continued, sometimes over weeks, until

---

[1] Sr. Benedicta Ward, SLG, *The Prayers and Meditations of Saint Anselm* (Middlesex, England: Penguin Books, 1984), 44.

the group felt certain that what they undertook was what God had called them to do. This provided a more solid foundation and a better motivation for what they planned to do later on.

Anselm's famous saying about "belief" placed relationships with God before action or even comprehension: "I believe so that I may understand."[1] Certain truths about God, he believed, could be grasped only after one had made a commitment to him. Action for him always grew out of the soil of his prayer.

I already sensed the truth of this, but Anselm's insistence upon prayer as the gateway to understanding was often reversed in my rush to achieve quick results: "The Christian ought to progress through faith to understanding, and not through understanding to faith,"[2] he wrote. Action taken without sufficient deliberation, however noble the cause, runs the risk of losing its way, as W. B. Yeats observed in his poem "The Second Coming."[3] The relationships I formed in Nativity parish gave me a much clearer reason for what I undertook and a point from which to plot my progress. The process was slower in time but much more lasting in commitment. Best of all, it was driven by faith and organic.

Conclusion:

In total, I have served in eight parishes, and in each one the people gave me far more theological insights than I gave them. I had many more years of formal training than they, but they had wisdom from a different source. Among the children especially I began to regain the gift of wonder that I seemed to have lost or even jettisoned down the

---

[1] Ward (244) quotes St. Anselm, "I do desire to understand your truth a little, that truth which my heart believes and loves. For I do not seek to understand so that I may believe, but I believe so that I may understand. And what is more, I believe that unless I do believe, I shall not understand. [*Desidero aliquatenus intelligere veritatem tuam, quam credit et amat cor meum. Neque enim quaero intelligere ut credam, sed credo ut intellegam. Nam hoc credo: quia nisi credidero, non intellegam*]." (Proslogion 1, lines 152-157)

[2] R. W. Southern, *Saint Anselm: A Portrait in a Landscape* (New York: Cambridge University Press, 1990), 123.

[3] "Turning and turning in the widening gyre / The falcon cannot hear the falconer; / Things fall apart; the center cannot hold; / Mere anarchy is loosed upon the world, / The blood-dimmed tide is loosed, and everywhere / The ceremony of innocence is drowned; / The best lack all conviction, while the worst / Are full of passionate intensity."

years: "To see a world in a grain of sand and heaven in a wild flower."[1] I envied them for keeping what I had glimpsed on that long-ago Christmas morning, the wonder of it all.

Perhaps chief among the gifts I received from the people were lessons in the importance of human relationships and an insistence on the primacy of one's relationship with God. These were not lessons they learned in textbooks. Theirs were lessons forged in the smithies of their own faith-filled lives. They did their theology in the midst of life; mine was mostly out of books.

---

[1] William Blake, from "Auguries of Innocence": "To see a world in a grain of sand, / And a heaven in a wild flower, / Hold infinity in the palm of your hand, / And eternity in an hour."

Cosmogenesis and Love:
A Cosmo/Geo/Archeo/Psycho/Spirito Inquiry
Pete Nelson
January 23, 2008

I am part of, I live in, I belong in a universe of incomprehensible immensity and depth, of beauty, divinity, and sacred mystery.

Some perceive this universe as more than the cosmos with a small "c," that which is tangible to the human senses, measurable. They perceive it also as the Kosmos with a capital "K." With this change they intend to distinguish between the physical, exterior nature of the cosmos, described especially though Western physics, and the Kosmos. This Kosmos points to and includes the interiority of the Universe. That interiority is the as yet immeasurable but intuitively knowable capacity that is also known as Spirit. In this perspective, Spirit is a fundamental, essential energy of the Universe. Unmeasurable as yet by Western physics, it is a primary animating force of cosmogenesis.

Cosmogenesis is the nanosecond-by-nanosecond emergence of an ever-new Universe, omnipresently unfolding out of all that precedes and enfolding back into all that is. Cosmogenesis has duration that exceeds any designation of time hypothesized by Western physics. It is not an unimportant fact that you, that I, are in constant change. We will not be the same persons who leave this gathering as those who started here. Cosmogenesis is creation.

To better grasp these concepts of cosmos, Kosmos, and cosmogenesis, it may be useful to identify and experience how we all are located throughout the Universe, I invite you to go on a journey with me, a journey which in one sense transcends that of any known astronaut, of any known spaceship exploration into our solar system.

We can map this journey together since we are literally journeying together. First, make a dot in the center of your sheet of paper. That represents where you are right now. Now, draw a small circle around that dot. That represents where you and we are sharing a space together. Now, another close circle around that. That is Scrooby lounge. Now, a circle around that for Pilgrim Place. Another circle for Claremont. Another circle for eastern Los Angeles County. Another for southern California. Another for North America. Another for the northern hemisphere. Another for Gaia, mother Earth, rotating on her axis every 24 hours. Another for spinning Gaia circling around the sun every 365 days. Another for the solar system at the edge of the Milky Way galaxy spinning at astronomical speeds. And so on.

What an incredible, remarkable journey you and I make every second of our existence.

I had picked up a pen and started this mapping at my kitchen table one evening some years ago with no coherent goal in mind. By the time I was done, I was seized by the ecstasy that came from knowing deeply and experientially that I was simultaneously in each of these places and spaces. For the first time in my life that I could remember, I was ushered beyond the illusory boundary of separateness across the threshold of interconnectedness and wholeness.

This realization of interconnectedness and wholeness opened me up to the sacred mystery, the divinity of the Universe that was revealed to me in mystical moments as a child and since. This experience increasingly becomes the background within which all I experience as foreground is integrated. I am simultaneously across the Universe while animating Spirit drives the ever newness of cosmogenesis. I am simultaneously present and ever changing. I am part of creation, still creating.

Despite the mapping of simultaneity that reveals omnipresence and wholeness, there is still the temptation for me to try to sneak in the illusory backdoor the enculturated ideas of permanence, of this here and that there. But cosmogenesis will not allow that. Cosmogenesis asserts that there is no beginning and no end. It asserts that creation is "nowever"—always has been, always will be a nanosecond-by-nanosecond unfolding and enfolding of the energies of the divine universe.

This cosmic grand opera elicits an unending set of questions, some of which are for me a manifestation of the sacred and divine.

1. What happens to the "I" of my enculturated, conventional self-understanding as I move my focus from "one circle of location" to another? Since "I" am part of this divine Universe constantly emerging, constantly creating, am I divinity emerging?

2. How does a deepening consciousness of being omni-connected transform both within me and outside me an increasingly complex and deepening connectedness?

3. Since I am part of the Kosmos, and Kosmos is constantly

emerging, how am I part of this emergence, creation? Am I co-creator of cosmogenesis in my expanding and deepening consciousness?

4. If I focus temporarily and arbitrarily on Gaia, Mother Earth, how am I both part of and affected by geological forces such as tectonic plate upthrusts, volcanic eruptions and tsunami redistribution of global nutrients? What happens to the human understanding of "destruction" in creation?

5. How am I to understand the complexification on Earth of a consciousness that is fundamental in Kosmos? And what becomes of my responsibility—the ability to respond—to be cognizant of and to participate in the deepening interpenetration of universal consciousness in the trajectory of human development? What will happen IF, in cosmogenesis, in creation, the present tensions about human gender are integrated, then transcended to a higher consciousness?

6. How does this deepening consciousness and co-creation transform my understanding of any anthropocentric bias in concepts such as creation, the garden of Eden and "God's chosen people?"

7. Would the conventionality of these and other questions be transformed were I to focus the pondering of them from the dot location in this room to the location of southern California, the Earth spinning on its axis, the solar system's place at the edge of the Milky Way Galaxy, or . . . ?

8. And finally, belonging in the Universe, I have the challenge of considering the requirements, the responsibilities of membership, of belonging in the Universe. What are the responsibilities of belonging in the Doing Theology group, Pilgrim Place, Claremont, the Milky Way Galaxy? As a member of the human species, what is my responsibility for the global climate crisis, and to whom and what is my responsibility?

LOVE

Cosmogenesis is creation, the ever new, ever now emergence of the universe out of the sacred mystery. And although there is constant change, there is variation and duration of that which emerges. This variation of duration is manifested, for instance, in the difference between the "life span" of the Himalayan peaks and the twenty-four-hour life span of the Mayfly. There is the distinction of duration between the slow accretion of coral that forms the immense barrier reef of Australia and the explosion of a stellar nebula millions of light years away, the simultaneous shape-shifting of the new out of the present and past.

I appreciate now the quandary that Pierre Teilhard de Chardin (the French Jesuit paleontologist who died on Easter, 1955) expressed in his short book, *The Hymn of the Universe*. He said of the mystic that he is one who is caught between his yearning for the permanent and knowing all the while there is none.

I believe that within cosmogenesis, the ever new emergence of the Universe speaks to this yearning for the permanent. That yearning is, in part, the yearning for love. I see Spirit as a primary animating force of cosmogenesis, of creation. I see love as the force of some developmental direction for cosmogenesis, some leading forwards toward, a beckoning. Not towards some Teilhardian teleological end point, an Alpha-and-Omega point, but to an ever-deepening of the interconnectedness of all. It is a process in which humans participate, entering into a relationship of co-creation. I can more clearly see the mystic's yearning for permanence while knowing there is none, if I momentarily bracket the emerging, deepening love to just the Earth.

bell hooks, in her book *All about Love, New Visions*, quotes M. Scott Peck's definition of love as "the will to extend one's self for the purpose of nurturing one's own or another's spiritual growth." Aha! Surely this definition is included in the love spoken about by such historical figures as Buddha, Confucius, and Jesus, and more contemporary figures such as Mother Teresa, Nelson Mandela, Gandhi, and Martin Luther King.

This, the nurturing towards my or another's spiritual growth, is what I experienced in the tender embrace of love of my grandmother. It is what I experienced in the cooing and cradling of my babies in my arms. It is what I experience when my fingers touch another in their joy and exuberance, their wounding and fear. It is what I know as I listen to the second movement of Mahler's Fifth Symphony. It is what I feel of the sun's atomic inferno radiating life-sustaining energies 24 hours a day and with no expectation of gratitude or reciprocity. It is what I experience on a star-studded night high in the Black Hills of South Dakota when I am drawn to the beyond out there, which is, paradoxically, the "in here."

I am still exploring how to act on the following belief. I believe that an emerging, deepening love in cosmogenesis is available to ALL. This love that includes the shape-shifters of life and death includes ALL: the fiery core of the Earth; its hardened mantle, the hydrosphere and stratosphere and all the life forms from the simplest single cell to the most complex; the solar system, the Milky Way Galaxy and . . .

My question is, how am I to transact with ALL applying Peck's definition of love: "the will to extend one's self for the purpose of nurturing one's own or another's spiritual growth?" Since I believe that emerging, deepening love is for ALL, how do I now interact with the rat and the cockroach, the venomous viper, the inmate sentenced for child rape, the developer who legally drains a swamp, the wounded and fearful, the "political terrorist?" And how do I love the moon, sun, solar system and the Milky Way Galaxy so that cosmogenesis and love are assisted and not resisted? How am I to be in right relationship? How am I to be the good neighbor?

How do I love myself, my whole, interconnected, interbeing, Universal Self in a culture that promotes self-loathing so that I am in danger of becoming merely a fragmented pawn in shallow, carnival allurement? How do I stay present as co-creator of cosmogenesis, the nowever emergence of the newever, of creation?

How do I love?

How do I become love?

Mysteries and Revelations
Henry Hayden
February 6, 2008

Part 1
Mysteries

I. Creation

Creation is an utter mystery. There are six billion humans on earth who had no say as to when, to whom and where they were born. How is it that I was born in 1918, in New England, to Yankee parents whose ancestors on both sides of the family came to Boston in the 1630s? I could have been born in Darfur, Dar es Salaam, Dresden, Calcutta, Santiago, Minsk, or Vancouver.

Not only is it a mystery when and to whom I was born, but the tenuous thread of life stretching back to the dim recesses of time speaks of a mystery beyond description. Our ancestors survived wars, plagues, natural disasters, and diseases, yet lived to pass on the seed of life from which I was born.

This mystery was intensified by a horrendous dream or rather, nightmare I had in the hospital in January 2006. I found myself bound head to foot in ropes, unable to move, and lying in the dark hold of a ship. Suddenly I was dragged down a plank, thrown on the ground, unbound, and yanked to my feet, struck several times in the face and yelled at in a language I didn't understand. I looked down at my thin arms and they were black. I was grabbed and thrown into a wagon with other young men and we rolled down a bumpy road, and suddenly I awoke with a scream.

This dream of being a bound slave was undoubtedly brought on by my post-operation high fever and total paralysis of my limbs. It gave me a horrifying glimpse of what it would have been like to have been born into another age and circumstance of life. It intensified the mystery of why I should have been born into a secure and loving family that shaped my unique identity.

The earth-bound time/space identity is eclipsed by the vast macro-universe in which we are enveloped. The earth is a small planet in the solar system; which is one among billions of similar systems. Yet the laws of motion, gravitation and electromagnetism are the same in the tiniest unit, the atom, as in the cosmos. All of this knowledge has been discovered in relatively recent times. Hence, the human intelligence receptor has seen itself as congruent with all creation.

I took organic evolution and several courses in geology in college in the 1930s, and my professors were avowedly atheist or agnostic, contrasting "scientific naturalism" as a superior answer to the naive literalism of the Genesis six-day creation.

Yet the creation story (possibly 4,000 years old) had the order of Earth's creation congruent with evolutionary science.

In a philosophy course with a Quaker professor, I was able to live comfortably with faith and evolutionary science. He often said, "The more we know, the more we know of God! Never be afraid of the quest for knowledge in any field."

II. The Mystery of Evil

Whence came animosities and violent expressions between individuals, clans, races, and nations often exacerbated by and intensified by religion?

I am sitting in a living room with seven other men on a peaceful summer afternoon. We are discussing how to cope with single life after the deaths of our wives. Our host has a small dachshund asleep on his lap.

Suddenly the dog awakes, his ears prick up, and he begins to bark furiously. He leaps to the floor and runs to the front door, barking louder and more threateningly. He is telling us "someone is invading my territory!" It is only the mailman.

Over almost 90 years of life, I have seen countless examples of human anger and defensiveness when some new person, idea, or group "invades my territory."

I remember the hostility shown to newcomers in our small, homogeneous town when newcomers who were "different" came to live, especially if they were Jewish or Roman Catholic.

I remember fights between public and parochial school students at the corner when the schools let out in the afternoon. This was in a small city where I lived between 1922-1929.

I remember the racial graffiti and broken windows when the first black family moved into our neighborhood in the 1950s in Fresno.

I remember the curses hurled at the migrant labor marchers as they march from Delano to Sacramento seeking fair wages, decent housing, and freedom from pesticides.

Is this deep-seated tendency to reject the "other," the different, a legacy of our animal nature, reaching back into the deep recesses of time? Is it our "original sin" that makes us instinctively put ourselves and our welfare first, and all others second? Our Puritan ancestors inscribed it in primary school text books. "In Adam's fall, we sinned all." It is a mystery that haunts us all.

III. The Mystery of Goodness

Baffling as are the mysteries of Creation and Evil, the persistence of Goodness (virtue, self-giving love, *agape*) is even more so. It is the tender plant that grows in the most unlikely places, and thrives when all seems lost. As we approach the Lenten season, we behold Love on a cross, the symbol of human rejection, enduring a death of shame. As the hymn says, "Yet that scaffold sways the future, and behind the dim unknown, standeth God within the shadows keeping watch above His own." (Lowell)

Our Old Testament heritage enshrines the prophets' lone voices extolling peace, reconciliation, recognition of our own complicity in evil.

We think of Amos reminding Israel that it would pay for its sins as would all the other nations who exploited the poor and went to war without cause.

Jeremiah crossed the enemy lines to speak with the General whose army was besieging Israel, and for this was cast down an abandoned well to die.

Isaiah held up a vision of peace and justice where the divisions of life would be healed and the lion would lie down with the lamb.

Embedded in Leviticus is the core of God's laws: "You shall love your neighbor as yourself." It is surrounded by a text which contains sacramental laws and duties. Love for neighbor is always in danger of being a love for the clan member who is like ourselves.

The gospels clearly extend the duty to love and care about the "other" to those in need of care, no matter who they are. The centuries betray a long and often futile attempt to put an inclusive *agape* kind of love into practice.

Within our lifetime we have seen several heroic figures challenge us to make love all inclusive: Albert Schweitzer, Dietrich Bonhoeffer, Anne Frank, Martin Luther King, Jr., Mother Theresa, President of South Africa Nelson Mandela, and others whom we do not know pushed the boundaries of human caring to greater circumference.

Even though every precept of my family, the teachers and

professors who supervised my education, the clergy of several churches, including my four years of College Chapel all seemed to convey to me "love your own kind," yet I was never satisfied with that, and always clung to the love portrayed in the Gospels. The desire to commune with the "other" was deep within my heart.

Part 2
Revelations

The following very personal revelatory experiences enabled me to deal with the three primary mysteries of which I have written:

Creation: How can I totally accept and rejoice in my small place in this mysterious overflowing stream of creation which is a manifestation of what we call God?

Evil: How did events in my life lead me from hatred and rejection of the "other" to embrace and reconcile with the "other"?

Good: How did certain events and people open my life to divine love, and the pursuit of a path of service and witness to divine love manifest in Christ?

Herewith are a very few of the many revelatory experiences that shaped my life!

I. Torture and Empathy

In 1928 Alfred Smith, Governor of New York, a Roman Catholic and a "wet" (wished to repeal 18th amendment) ran for President of the United States against Herbert Hoover, a Quaker. This political contest unleashed hostile emotions in Protestant and Roman Catholic citizens.

My father, like dozens of other Connecticut Yankees, was recruited to join a newly formed chapter of the Ku Klux Klan. In post-Civil War Reconstruction days this was largely anti-Negro, designed to suppress newly freed slaves. But in the 1920s, it was designed to suppress Catholics, Jews, and "foreigners" (recent immigrants).

My father, (8th grade, one room school educated) quickly rose to be Kleagle in the Rockville, Connecticut chapter, spent nights burning crosses on Fox Hill above the small mill-town city, and weekends attending Klan rallies in fields adjacent to rural farms.

When parochial school students learned of my father's role in those anti-catholic intimidating activities, they kidnaped me, a small 10-year-old, on my way home from public school, took me to the woods above Bradley field, tied me to a tree with ropes from "head to foot," took off my shoes and socks and stubbed out their cigarettes on the bottoms of my feet. My screams alarmed them as they heard people coming through the woods. They ran off and left me there for several hours until a farmer's wife heard my cries for help and released me.

This experience was a trauma that lasted for years, and gave me empathy for all victims of torture and violence. And it ensures my participation in Amnesty International.

II. Compassion

My roommate, David and I lived on the 3rd floor of Jarvis Hall at Trinity College in Hartford in the spring of 1936. On the first floor lived George, a polio victim, on crutches, with a small, dwarfed body. He stood in his doorway day after day, and we rushed by him with a hasty "Hi, George!"

One night I came in late and found my roommate waiting to talk with me. "Henry, tonight I stopped to talk with George, went into his room, and visited for almost an hour! But before I left he told me that he was desperately lonely, and that if he did not make a friend before Easter vacation, when he went home to Danbury, he would kill himself. I think he really meant it!"

We talked for hours, devised a plan to bring him in touch with our own circle of friends, take him out to Saturday night dinner at a local diner, accompany us on track team bus trips, and try to get him on the school newspaper staff since he had done this activity in High School.

Our plan worked, George became our friend, we came to know his wise and witty personality, and in 1939 his parents, in gratitude, loaned us their car to take George to New York's World's Fair.

III. Futility

I am an employee! No small accomplishment in the last year of the depression. I am a clerk at the Hartford Fire Insurance Company home office. With the magnificent salary of $1,500 a year, I have a desk and a dictating machine with removable rolls to take to the stenographic department where my letters to agents are transcribed. Before me each day are immense stacks of DRs (carbon copies of issued policies called "Daily Reports").

Around me are 20 or 30 similar desks, occupied by older men, mostly married with children. The work is repetitive and deadly boring, not much better than the 16 jobs I did to earn my way through college. My fellow workers with whom I eat lunch confess their boredom and hatred of their work. They feel "trapped," and tell me they try to get drunk on weekends to erase the boredom of their work.

Their conversations and their plight raise a red flag in my mind. I resign after six months, and go to Syracuse University to pursue an M.A. in English. I feel life work should be a passion, not just making a living.

IV. Mentoring/Shepherding

It is June 10, 1939 and I have my B.A. degree in English Literature. After four years of struggle to stay in school with little or no money and working part-time throughout the four years, I look forward to "rest and relaxation" until I start my new job as a budding Insurance Executive, which my father assures me I will become someday and "own a $10,000 house in West Hartford."

But upon arriving home, I find my father has promised me to YMCA Camp Woodstock as a camp counselor for six weeks! I am furious, but remembering my dad's sacrifices in helping me through college, I grudgingly agreed to accept the assignment. I was the last counselor to arrive at camp only to find I had been assigned the cabin with 15 boys from an orphanage (on scholarship) who were "tough, troublesome and belligerent." They had no mothers or fathers, lived in large dormitories in a Dickensian old brick institution. They were my responsibility for six weeks!

In the period I became an elder brother/father/friend to each one, taught them sport skills, led in nightly devotions, took them on overnight hikes, and helped them achieve "best cabin" award! That mentoring was so deeply rewarding that it pointed me to my ultimate vocation.

V. My Mentor, A Task, Fulfillment

In fall of 1940, I pursued my M.A. in English at Syracuse University and accepted a part-time job weekends to pay my educational costs. I signed with The Reverend Alfred H. Rapp of Plymouth Congregational Church in the center of downtown Syracuse to be program director for Junior High, Senior High and College-age groups of the church. The friendship of the Rev. Mr. Rapp, and his personal guidance and direction made this a turning point in my life. At the end of the year I had decided on seminary, found a wife in that congregation, and set out for California.

VI. Encountering Poverty

My summer job upon arriving in the Bay area was providing recreation for minor children of migrant laborers in the Sonoma Valley. This was the summer when I saw poverty first-hand—people living in shacks, sleeping on the floor on newspapers, water faucets at an outdoor location at the end of each row of shacks. When workers came stumbling out of a long row of crops where insecticide had been sprayed while they worked, they were coughing and crying. I spoke to the field boss about it. His reply was, "Yes they cough their lungs out, but we get a new bunch of pickers next year." These people were the Okies and Arkies who had fled the dust bowl, and who were immortalized in John Steinbeck's *Grapes of Wrath*. This was an experience from which I had been sheltered all my life—it left me "radicalized."

VII. The Muilenburg Experience

Seminary shook up all my assumptions about the Bible, life, politics, and the church. But of all the faculty who challenged and inspired me, no one had a greater effect on my whole life than Dr. James Muilenburg. He guided us through the prophets for whom he had a passion and profound respect. Amos, Micah, Jeremiah, and Isaiah (both "First" and "Second") came alive to us. He desired to make us all prophets, willing to "tell truth to power," challenge the comfortable and the indifferent, identify with the poor, the outcasts, and the disenfranchised. "Don't preach a lot of 'saccharine pap!'" he would say at the end of a lecture. I believed him in a naive and uncritical way, and set out upon my ministry destined to be in "divine trouble" for almost 50 years.

VIII. Other Revelatory Experiences

Through the years doors opened and new prophets alien to my previous experience appeared. Herewith are a few of those experiences:

1. Sitting at a table in an African-American minister's home late at night and talking to the Rev. Martin Luther King, Jr.
2. Joining the march from Delano to Sacramento led by César Chávez.
3. Joining the "Brother to Brother" movement and adopting prisoners at San Quentin who were to be discharged in a few months. This meant monthly visits to the prison, and securing housing and jobs for them upon release.

4. Shepherding seminary student William Johnson through the "coming out" process in my San Carlos church one month after I had been called to that pastorate. He revealed his homosexual orientation to 15 members of my Board of Deacons on October 1, 1970 and they voted unanimously to recommend his ordination. Since the Northern California Conference Committee on the Ministry took a negative view of our decision, they recommended two years of study of the sexuality issues. We took the challenge, preached and had forums monthly until finally an ordaining council was called June 10, 1972 and William Johnson was affirmed by a 2 to 1 margin by the 169 voting delegates. The degree of hatred encountered in this quest far outstripped my expectations. You were right, Dr. Muilenburg, being a prophet isn't easy.

IX. Near Fatal Illness

On December 16, 2005 I had five vertebrae operated on at Cedars-Sinai Hospital. It seemed successful and I came home January 1, 2006. Within a short time I was overcome with a massive streptococcus infection and spent several weeks in Pomona Valley Hospital, and awoke from a coma to find myself virtually paralyzed. I begged to be allowed to die, but my daughter and my doctor talked me out of that decision, and urged me to "fight my way back" to a more normal life. This experience brought me face to face with mortality, and taught me to intensely treasure each day as a priceless gift.

Conclusion

In Thornton Wilder's American classic *Our Town*, the play concludes with a scene in which the character Emily (who has died in childbirth in the previous act) pleads with the Stage Manager (representing God) to be allowed to return to earth for a single day. He warns her that this is not wise and would be too painful, but she pleads with him until he relents, and she returns to relive the day of her 12th birthday. As the scene unfolds, she watches her family go about their daily life unaware of the tragedies that lie in the future. Suddenly, she runs from the scene, appalled by the way her brother and parents behave, crying out, "I can't. I can't go on. . . . Do any human beings ever realize life while they live it—every, every minute?"

Having had a "near death" experience, I have resolved to live every moment of my remaining days with a sense of wonder and awe at the beauty of each moment, each person, each sunrise, and each sunset, and to waste no moment in vain regrets of the past, or vain hopes for the future.

My Theological Journey
Ruth M. Harris
February 20, 2008

MY WESLEYAN ROOTS

I was born in Nebraska into a family of Methodists. My grandfather was a Methodist minister and was a veteran of the Civil War. He and my grandmother Clara migrated from New York State to be in mission on the frontier. In Nebraska, the Rev. George F. Cole preached in many rural communities and started new churches. Clara Cole worked beside him and was also active in the Woman's Suffrage Movement and the Woman's Christian Temperance Union. She and Esther, their youngest daughter, my mother, were major influences on my life.

From childhood I attended church with my family, and we children sang in the choir, went to church school and camp, and took an active part in church activities. It was not surprising that I heard the challenge to be in mission sitting alone in my home church: "Love God with all your heart and soul and mind and strength, and your neighbor as yourself." That seriousness about living the faith led me to become a Methodist missionary in China.

John Wesley had been a reformer in the Church of England in the 18th century. He and his brother Charles were called Methodists in Oxford University because of their disciplined lives and searching spirits. Wesley's concern about poor and working people, about literacy and education, about health and justice led him to activities outside the confines of the church and into the fields and the city streets. Eventually the Methodist Church grew out of this new soil and took root in Britain and in the United States as an independent movement.

Furthermore, Methodism has emphasized inclusivity, offering the right hand of fellowship to one and all, and toning down dogma and rigid tests for membership. It has been an open community and has invited members to rely on their own thinking and conscience. What Methodists call "the quadrilateral," defining sources of faith as scripture, reason, tradition, and experience, opens options, including, very importantly, believers' own journeys of mind and heart.

Methodists have been a singing people, and the hymns of Charles Wesley have been a rich legacy. They have given Wesleyan theology in clear and compelling form. "O For a Thousand Tongues to Sing," "Come, Thou Long-Expected Jesus," "Hark! The Herald Angels

Sing," "Christ the Lord Is Risen Today," "Love Divine, All Loves Excelling," "A Charge to Keep I Have," "Jesus, Lover of My Soul." These are but a few of the inspiring and theologically educative hymns he wrote. Singing Sunday after Sunday I absorbed the spirit and the message.

PEOPLE POWER IN CHINA

I went to China in 1947 and lived there for four years, two years before Mao Tse Tung came to power, and two years after. I will never forget the shock of poverty that I saw as our ship docked at the Shanghai wharf. Small boats crowded around our ship carrying Chinese with arms outstretched begging for anything the passengers on deck above would throw down to them. As we landed, we were immediately surrounded by a large crowd begging us to use their services, carrying baggage, pulling pedicabs. As we walked along the jammed streets, we saw huge wagons piled high and drawn by human beings rather than animals.

A week later I traveled by a small Chinese ship north to Tianjin and then to Beijing to study Chinese language. The language school brought together English-speaking people from many countries who were coming to live in China, representing businesses, governments and religions. This international community lived and studied together. I was asked to teach Chinese songs for one hour each week to the language school student body. These songs chosen by the young Chinese faculty were 'liberation songs' which were then emerging in north China. There was nothing in their texts that we did not sing with gusto.

With friends I went to the countryside and provincial towns. Gradually the whole country was divided into study groups which focused on the reform and improvement of the country and self-examination of bourgeois attitudes and actions that impeded change. Here I first heard university students engage in "criticism-self-criticism" and express their outrage at the encroachment of foreign powers. For the first time I realized that one of those imperial powers was my own country.

In Shanghai I taught choral music at a Methodist girls' high school. After Mao's army arrived in 1949, it seemed that everyone in Shanghai in factories, schools and all institutions was involved in a carefully designed educational process. We studied the goals of the new government, such as land reform, medical care, reeducation, support for peasants and workers. I was amazed at the changes in my school. Girls who had been stylish now wore common dress. Faculty and student leaders expressed their support for radical change. I saw with my own eyes the beginning of transformation in a society that needed desperately to change.

With the coming of the Communists to Shanghai, there was a significant change in the school toward Christians. Previously there had been compulsory weekly chapel which brought all the students and faculty together in the large auditorium. This service could no longer be held. Every student was required to attend a class on the goals and policies of the new government. In these classes each student had to share her own progress in relation to politics and faith. Instead of chapel a new church was organized at the school. Led by our former chaplain, it included any teachers and students who wished to attend, as well as Christians in the neighborhood.

A Chinese teacher and I were sponsors of a youth fellowship on Sunday afternoons. It became a significant time for all of us as new challenges confronted us daily. Discussing what it means to be a Christian, our fellowship became very lively. As we sang hymns, the words suddenly became very personal and deeply meaningful. For me the church became real in a way that I had never experienced before. I recall missionary friends who came to visit me as they were returning to the United States. They inquired about my well-being. I assured them that I had never felt better and that I was experiencing "the church alive."

It was not until the United States and China were at war at the Yalu River on the North Korean border that it became too uncomfortable for my friends to have me remain in China. At my last Christmas I sang the "Messiah" with an all-Chinese choir. Ringing in my ears were the words: "For unto us a child is born, unto us a son is given, and the government shall be upon his shoulder, and his name shall be called Wonderful, Counselor, the mighty God, the everlasting Father, the Prince of Peace." In early 1951 I left China with deep regret, looking for some way to reconcile and build peace. As I walked across the border to Hong Kong, I felt a strong conviction that had been growing within me: that God uses people power.

On my way home friends and I traveled through parts of southern Asia, the Middle East, and Europe. In Geneva I was able to attend the United Nations' sessions led by Eleanor Roosevelt and Charles Malik to draft the "Declaration of Human Rights." Having been cut off from news in China, I began to understand the exciting developments at the United Nations. As soon as I reached New York City, I applied to work for the UN. No luck. "Many applicants. You are overqualified." Instead I worked for the women of the United Methodist Church educating church people from all over the country who came to New York. Eleanor Roosevelt became one of our resource people for UN seminars.

Later I worked on the staff of the National Student Christian Federation, and then as Methodist Women's national secretary of student work. In response to Dr. Martin Luther King's call, a colleague and I went to Selma for a couple of weeks to march and work in organizing. I joined in efforts to enable students and campus ministers who came from around the country to take part in the Civil Rights struggle. In the midst of the danger and intensity of those days, I was once again amazed at the power and vision of people to transform society. The black churches and congregations were essential bases for the movement. Preaching and singing inspired each day and night's activity. Dr. Martin Luther King, Jr. and his followers provided incredible leadership. In naming God and the Christian faith as the foundation for the justice struggle, King's liberation theology inspired one of the most important movements the United States has ever seen. Never had I been more convinced that God works through people power.

LIBERATION THEOLOGY

In September 1985, in a time of escalating violence in South Africa due to the apartheid system, 151 Christians from more than 20 denominations published a remarkable document called "Challenge to the Church: A Theological Comment on the Political Crisis in South Africa." Developing out of widely held grassroots discussions and involving clergy and lay people, this became known as "The Kairos Document."

The Kairos Document was circulated among churches, especially in the developing world. Christians in seven different countries found these words so compelling about the suffering of South Africans and so relevant to their own struggles that they engaged in dialogue for two and a half years and then joined in signing a statement that they called "The Road to Damascus: Kairos and Conversion." In the Preamble, they wrote:

> We, the signatories of this document, are Christians from different Church traditions in seven different nations: the Philippines, South Korea, Namibia, South

Africa, El Salvador, Nicaragua, and Guatemala. What we have in common is not only a situation of violent political conflict, but also the phenomenon of Christians on both sides of the conflict. This is accompanied by the development of a Christian theology that sides with the poor and oppressed and the development of a Christian theology that sides with the oppressor. This is both a scandal and a crisis that challenges the Christian people of our countries.

Although the phenomenon is much the same in each of our countries, the two antagonistic forms of Christianity are referred to with a variety of names: liberation theology, black theology, feminist theology, minjung theology, theology of struggle, the Church of the poor, the progressive church, basic Christian communities, on the one hand; and the religious right, right-wing Christianity, state theology, the theology of reconciliation, the neo-Christendom movements and anticommunist evangelicals on the other hand. In each of our nations we will have to spell out exactly which groups of Christians we are referring to. Whatever differences of terminology there may be, the conflict and division among Christians is basically the same in each of our countries.

The time has come for us to take a stand and to speak. The road ahead is like the road to Damascus along which Saul was traveling to persecute the first generation of Christians. It was along this road that he heard the voice of Jesus calling him to conversion. We are all in continuous need of self-criticism and conversion. But now the time has come for a decisive turnabout on the part of those groups and individuals who consciously or unconsciously compromised their Christian faith for economic and selfish purposes.

It was in this context that I spent my years as an executive of the World Division, United Methodist Board of Global Ministries, especially during the last fifteen years under the title of Secretary for Global Justice. I was related to peoples' movements: urban, rural, student, antiwar and peace, sustainability, anti-racist, and feminist movements. I had the amazing opportunity to travel all over the world, especially in the global south. My work was not only denominational but broadly ecumenical and sometimes interfaith as well. Especially meaningful was participation in the leadership of Agricultural Missions, the World Student Christian Federation, and the Church Coalition for Human Rights in the Philippines.

During the Marcos military dictatorship representatives of US Catholic and Protestant churches worked in solidarity with church and secular movements in the Philippines on issues of human rights, US military bases, poverty, and American foreign policy in support of oppression. I was profoundly moved by the courage and vision of priests and ministers, nuns and deaconesses, as well as other organizers, who risked life and imprisonment to stand with oppressed people. At the same time we were confronting oppressive forces and the churches who supported or did not stand up to them.

During my decade as chairperson of the Church Coalition for Human Rights in the Philippines, I became particularly interested in what Filipinos called "theology of struggle." The August 1972 Declaration of Christians for National Liberation lists their tasks as: recognizing the collusion of external neocolonialism and internal domination of elites; seeking to work for national liberation and economic sovereignty; affirming that the churches must decide where they will stand between the elite and the working masses; and taking on the mission of exposing oppression, organizing for struggle, and purging themselves of selfishness and pride in order to serve the people.

Christianity, the Declaration says, has a liberating message, calling people to freedom and salvation. This is not pie-in-the-sky but liberation as a human and collective task, announcing a new humanity but without endorsing any one ideology or program. It rejects the ways that the official churches have "knowingly or unknowingly collaborated with the present ruling powers, and have been used in the cultural subjugation of our people."

Christians for National Liberation conclude: "We commit ourselves to revolutionary ecumenism, to self-criticism and criticism, together with other organized groups. We shall make special efforts to overcome dogmatism and Christian triumphalism in our relationship with the Muslims, other cultural minorities, and the Marxists. We make this declaration with a deep sense of repentance for having been too reluctant and slow in responding to the signs of the times."

My experience as a first world Christian in solidarity brought me face to face with poverty and repression. My work was to be an advocate for justice, often confronting my own country's policies, as in the case of U. S. military bases and multinational economic control in the Philippines. Both within the United States and internationally, I saw the struggle of the two churches, one for the oppressed, the other supporting the oppressor, both calling themselves Christian. In a speech I gave in a conference in Mindanao, I began with a poem by an Australian aboriginal woman.

> If you have come to help me
> you are wasting your time
> But if you have come
> because your liberation
> Is bound up with mine,
> then let us work together.

I knew that our liberations were bound together. My Christian faith was often tested, but I was clear as to whose side I was on.

COMING TO CLAREMONT AND PROCESS THEOLOGY

Coming to Claremont has been an exciting adventure in deepening and broadening my theology. Process Theology, grounded in the philosophy of Alfred North Whitehead, has offered me a way to bring together the strands of theology that have influenced me through my lifetime and to find a more comprehensive understanding of faith and life. The inspiration of the thinking of John B. Cobb, Jr., Marjorie Suchocki, David Ray Griffin, and others has pushed me toward clarity and integration. The way that Process takes seriously the Christian faith and the way it relates to science, aesthetics, interreligious understanding, and moral and ethical issues, has been exciting and freeing for me. What surprised me is that I began to hear answers to questions I didn't realize I was asking. Process has offered a way to integrate the challenges and concerns of life with a view of God as luring us toward a transformed future and moving along the way with us.

As a very busy activist and executive, I did not spend much time analyzing exactly what I believed. My Christian commitment to justice and peace was firm; my constant interaction with people in struggle was nourishing and inspiring. Among the speakers related to the Process Center, something Marjorie Suchocki said within ten days after 9/11 grabbed my attention. She was speaking on the problem of evil, and someone asked her what she thought had happened to the hijackers. She said that God never gives up on anyone. She said that God would continue to work with them no matter how long it would take. Her words really confronted me with how God reaches out to us, is reaching out to me. I realized that I needed to think through more carefully what I believe about God. Much of our faith is shaped by the kind of God we believe in.

I became really excited when I read David Ray Griffin's *Two Great Truths: A New Synthesis of Scientific Naturalism and Christian Faith*. Before discussing the distortions in science and faith that keep them apart, he outlines his "Eight Primary Doctrines of the Christian Good News." I find his articulation of the heart of the Christian faith exciting, succinct, and true to my convictions as well.

1. Our world has been created by a good, loving, wise, purposive God.
2. God, loving all of us, desires that we treat each other with justice and compassion.
3. Our world is essentially good, even though it is now full of evil.
4. God continues to act in the world, especially through human beings, to foster good and overcome evil.
5. God's love, concern for justice, and purpose, having already been expressed through a series of prophets and sages, were revealed in a decisive way through Jesus of Nazareth.
6. The divine purpose, thus revealed, is to overcome evil by bringing about a "reign of God" on earth, in which the present subjugation of life to demonic values (lies, ugliness, injustice, hate, and indifference) will be replaced by a mode of life based on divine values (truth, beauty, goodness, justice, and compassion).
7. Salvation can be enjoyed here and now, at least in a partial way, through direct experience of, and empowerment by, God as Holy Spirit, and by the faith that, no matter what, our lives have ultimate meaning, because nothing can separate us from the love of God.
8. The divine purpose is also to bring about an even more complete salvation in a life beyond bodily death.

Furthermore, I have been impressed with the work of Process theologians as they have analyzed the economic, military, and political dimensions of American Empire and sought to imagine just and peaceful alternatives.

Long interested in China, I am inspired by the dialogue between American process thinkers and Chinese officials and academicians. They have a remarkable exchange occurring around eco-civilization, key values for the post-modern era, including how they are related to Chinese traditional thought, and concrete ways to imagine modernization without falling into the destructive economic, environmental, and cultural patterns of the West.

What Claremont has provided for me is a chance to step back from struggle to reflect and learn more. I am not putting away past theological insights, but God is luring me on. All that I have learned and known is now in a broader framework. Some liberation theology, to which I was attracted, was sexist and neglected nature. One key is that whereas in the past much of what I was looking at was human-centered, I need a broader, more comprehensive view of the whole of life and the creation. This is not otherworldly, but an attempt to encompass all aspects of life. I welcome the openness that Process Theology offers to engagement with people of other religions. I keep on learning day by day, and I am deeply grateful that I have come to Claremont.

One last word of appreciation is for the Pilgrim Place community. Within this small town family, we can draw strength and wisdom and can support each other as we continue to work for the common good and seek to grow in faith, perfection in love, and response to God's continual urging toward the good, beautiful, just, and compassionate.

Six Letters to Our Grandchildren:
Be All That You Are!

Jim Lamb

March 5, 2008

#1

Hi Gabriel & Isabella!

A few months ago, when my 80th birthday came and went, as did your 7th birthdays, I had the urge to write. And so I began these letters—some short, some longer—written to you and hoping you would not mind my sharing them with some friends.

I have placed your photo at the top of this collection because you help me think, and wonder, and pray. You ask important questions, speak honestly about worries; you never stop being excited about learning. So much in our great Cosmos we adults cannot yet understand—but your power of imagination seems to have grown more each time Grandma and I see you!

Gabriel and Isabella, you were born only six days apart but very soon you became much more than cousins—you became best friends, even though many miles then separated you. I regret now that I was never good friends with my cousins.

I have much to learn from you and perhaps you might learn some things from me. Actually, I have a strong belief that "dialogical learning" is often the best, most fun way to see new things or to solve problems. Probably you know the beautiful word "dialog" means to talk together, to exchange ideas. Certainly you understand the idea because

VOLUME III

Grandma and I so often see your parents dialoging with you and each other. And when we visited your schools, we saw you and your classmates sitting in small circles with the teacher, each student listening, then speaking. How encouraging for us!

Did your parents or Uncle Chris ever tell you about our "Family Meetings?" Well, once the youngest member reached age 8 or 9, we began to sit together whenever the family needed to plan something, like a vacation trip. Or whenever someone was upset or angry. Any one of us could call a meeting, not only a parent. I believe now, many years later, that experience was an important reason why we still learn from each other, and why our mutual love grows and grows.

Anyhow, I learned even more about the possibilities of "dialogical learning" when Grandma and I became good friends with a Brazilian family, especially the mother and father, Paulo & Elza Freire. I began to better understand the importance of speaking that favored "we" rather than "I" or "me" or "mine." I've noticed how you do that in school, and how when a classmate distracts the group, that kid is given a peaceful "time out."

Since you both love books, you will be pleased to know that Paulo later became world-famous with the publication of his most famous book in many languages.[1] That book explains how poor children, who had to work and could not go to school, can later learn to read and write anyway, and become what we lucky adults call "literate." However, they learn in ways that make them proud and braver, because they also learn to read their lives as well as books and newspapers.

Gabriel, sometimes when you and I were constructing skyscrapers with Legos I thought about Paulo teaching people who were "illiterate" and supposedly "without words" or ideas.[2] Your ideas came from your knowledge and your mind. In the beginning theirs only came from what they saw in their lives every day. So when they talked with each other, and Paulo, and began to also make words, they realized they could also build better lives for their families. They became People of Hope. And Isabella, they did this with the excitement that comes from dialogue and new learning.

If you find this way of learning interesting, we can talk about it. You have ideas about making words. I think that you and Paulo would

---

[1] Paulo Friere, *Pedagogy of the Oppressed* (Herder & Herder, 1970).

[2] Ana Maria Araujo Freire & Donaldo Macedo, *The Paulo Freire Reader* (Continuum, 1998).

have become very good friends!

Isabella, as I look at your photo I remember how much you love dance and gymnastics, and your marvelous ability to straddle doorways and hallways—and even raise yourself to ceilings. Too, your thirst for reading and your joy when playing teacher with Grandma and me as your eager students!

Gabriel, you seem to love math and architecture and adventure. In the photo you wear the shirt with the words "Helicopter Rescue Mission," and so you have already saved many helpless people in your imagination. I'm sorry the photo only shows the wooden sword you made, and not also the shield you carved in school. Right, knights promised to use them to protect people in need.

Anyway, my exciting young friends, people of all ages and nations need encouragement and ideas to be whatever God has put in us to be.

You make my heart smile. I'll be writing more.

Love always,
Grandpa

#2

Dear Gabriel & Isabella,

I am so pleased that you both often talk with your Moms and Dads about challenges in your school work and many other important things. For example, Gabriel, your Mom was telling me about your concern that there are so many homeless people. And that earlier you said something like this:

Mom, I'm worrying about some things. Maybe too
much. There is so much that is a mystery to me. I guess
my life is a journey to find answers.

I think your insight—your inner sight—sharing is wonderful! I don't say "wonderful" because it is a nice word. I wrote it because your spirit and your search are wonder-full. I hope you will never, never cease to be in awe of how much there is to learn!

Isabella and Gabriel, have you ever listened to the Irish singer Enya? She once wrote a lovely song called "Pilgrim." The final lyrics repeat, "It's a long way to find out who you are . . . It's a long way to find out who you are." Well, twice a month I sit in a circle of friends—20 or more—here at Pilgrim Place. We agree that our lives have been journeys filled with discoveries and questions. So we often talk about things that still puzzle us.

You are 7 years old. We Pilgrims are at least ten times older but still intrigued by mysteries that remain mysteries. We worry sometimes but maybe the only mistake would be to worry alone, especially because there are so many good people who care about us.

Personally I think that one of the greatest mysteries is: What happens to people when they die and no longer live on this earth? Sure, we know that God loves us but exactly what will happen? I know that my parents, your great-grandparents who died long ago, are somehow still with me. I can't see them but I feel their presence. But what are they doing, and where?

Here is one possibility, and there must be many.

Emilia Rose, two days before her recent 4th birthday, completed an interesting picture puzzle. I was her cheerleader. She looked at it for a moment, then said, "I wish I was in the puzzle!" Naturally I asked, "Where in the puzzle?" Now the puzzle was filled with comfy teddy bears resting on clouds in a lovely star-filled sky, but without hesitation she put her finger on a bigger bear leaping from star to star!

"Why Emilia, why?" I asked. Her immediate response was, "Because I would love to jump from star to star!" I was so grateful to her! I had almost forgotten something very important.

You may know the Bible story when Jesus tells a group of adults—probably including some grandparents: "Unless you change and become as little children . . ." Well, you guys, not so little any more, are such an amazing source of creative and spiritual energy! Emilia Rose had to remind me that we live on a beautiful but tiny dot in the sky, called Planet Earth, whereas the joyful exuberance of God created a vast Cosmos with millions and millions of stars we might explore after we no longer live here!

Well, that's just one possibility: Death is a jumping off point! There is so much wonder to wonder about!

Love always,
Grandpa

#3

Dear Gabriel & Isabella,

When we were visiting last time I forgot to ask if either of you ever told Emelia that the body of every person in the world is made from material that comes from the stars, as well as water. Scientists have known that for a long time but probably not when I was in the first grade. You guys are so lucky!

Anyhow Isabella, some weeks ago your Dad told me about an important question you asked. He was so pleased it's now printed on the family BLOG so friends can also appreciate it.

Isabella: "Is God invisible?
Daddy: "Yes, God is invisible and everywhere."
Isabella: "What happens if I am walking around and I bump into God by accident?"
Daddy: "I think God likes it when you bump into him."

Your Dad was so right! In fact your "bumping question" takes me to another wonderment. In church a priest had just finished leading a "dialogue Mass"—meaning that anyone who wished could immediately discuss his sermon when he finished—and a young man asked, "Father, have YOU ever seen God?" WOW! What a fantastic question!

The priest was very quiet for a long time. Then he said, "Yes, I saw God yesterday." The priest explained that he had visited a very sad man in the local hospital several times. He discovered that the man might not get well because he was so depressed. He had not seen his only child in many years because they were angry with each other. "But yesterday," said the priest, "when I entered the sad man's room he and his son were laughing and hugging and laughing. Yes! I have seen God."

I think we bump into God, we see God all the time. If we pay attention. Because God is especially about Love. I haven't forgotten, Gabriel, that when you last visited here I asked what the word "God" meant to you. You thought a moment and then said, "To me it means Love."

My Pilgrim friends who sit in our big circle share marvelous stories, often talking about God's love. And experiencing it in all parts of this country and everywhere in this world. But I have not yet told them this other hospital story. It's about when you were born, Gabriel.

When you were still inside your Mom's tummy it seemed like you could not come out. She was therefore in great pain for a long, long time. Your Dad and Grandma and I tried hard to comfort her but the pain was terrible though she was very brave. I wonder how many in the very large hospital "receiving room" grew afraid like I did? More and more doctors and nurses kept joining us. The silence in the room, except for your Mom's moans, was intense.

Then suddenly we could see your emerging head. Then all of you: Gabriel was with us!! The room erupted with cheers and tears of joy and relief. And Grandma stepped forward to snip your life-line to your Mom, your umbilical cord, which you no longer needed!

Even as I tell both of you about that magnificent moment my eyes fill with tears. I felt the presence of God. I felt lifted off my feet. I felt embraced. I'll never, never forget what happened.

So, I think that very special "bumping into God" can occur as a surprise. Other times when we find ourselves in situations that turn out to be scary—like at Gabriel's birth. Maybe sometimes when we choose to risk doing the right thing or take a chance to help someone. Since you have recently been learning about Dr. Martin Luther King and the Civil Rights Movement, if you would like it, during your next visit I could invite some of my Pilgrim friends to tell you stories about adventures with him and very special "bumpings into God"!

Like when long ago some of us were with him in a city called Selma, in Alabama. In that state only white Americans were allowed to vote. Even if black Americans had won medals for bravery in serving their country. Can you even imagine such unfairness?

Well, some friends and I joined hundreds of white and black Americans from all across this lovely country, to become like an awesome rainbow that finally could not be ignored.[1] Some angry local white men called us nasty names, carried guns or clubs, and held the leashes of vicious dogs. Sure, they made us afraid. But over and over we sang that beautiful song you have heard, "We Shall Overcome." We prayed, we held hands tightly, we marched, young people and old people together. Fifty years later I can still feel us, we of many colors and churches and cities, holding hands. We all felt God's presence together.

---

[1] Charles E. Fager, *Selma 1965: The March That Changed the South* (Beacon Press, 1974).

Emilia might ask, "I wonder how many stars touched when you joined hands in Selma?" Probably only God could answer that question.

Love always,
Grandpa

#4

Dear Gabriel & Isabella,

Last summer Grandma and I were sitting quietly on the southern shore of beautiful Lake Tahoe. Suddenly wild ducks landed in the water close by. We watched in amazement as one walked steadily toward us, closer and closer, until he (she?) settled down by my right side.

Let's give him sort of a Native American name: ONE WHO TRUSTS OTHERS.

Well, ONE made himself comfortable just below where my right hand rested on the chair arm. Before long he did a "duck thing." He tucked his head under one wing and went to sleep!

The lake became a place of enchantment, the three of us resting together in a magic place, a tiny place, cozy somewhere in God's vast Cosmos. We did not speak or move for a long time. Finally, when Grandma and I had to leave, ONE rose also as we regretfully waved farewell: farewell.

I tell you this lovely story because I am learning that you and I have, and maybe everyone has, important stories and surprises and questions to share. Most, but not all, will be happy.

Here's another happy one.

Isabella, one day just before sister Michaela's 4th birthday, she bounced onto my lap while I was sitting quietly on your living room couch. Blue eyes laughed into startled blue eyes as she announced importantly: "Grandpa, you're old!" Of course she was right, exactly right. Somehow her news made me feel good, very good. Someone told me Grandparents must become old before they can become Elders but I'm not entirely sure that I entirely understand the difference.

I'm trying hard to learn so I recently read an interesting book by a medical doctor entitled, *What Are Old People For?: How Elders Will*

Save the World.[1] His ideas are excellent but I think more can be added. Grandma and I are old but how can we become Elders and do more to help save the world?

Maybe some time soon when we talk you and Gabriel can give us some good ideas!

My first letter was too long. Probably you like this one better. Anyway, when you visit Lake Tahoe again watch for ONE, another very special new friend!

Love always,
Grandpa

#5

Hi Gabriel & Isabella,

As you know, Grandma was confined to hospitals for more than a month. She is a brave Mom's mom who here at home, with good doctors advising, works very hard every day to win better health. Thanks for all your phone calls and drawings and prayers. They help lots!

In the hospitals many staff members spoke Spanish, or Spanish and English. Like Grandma, you both already know some Spanish. Isn't it a special feeling to speak English well but also know other languages! When you are older I hope you choose to read a famous Spanish writer with a funny last name: Ortega y Gassett. He once said, "The will to be oneself is heroism. Life is a desperate struggle to be in fact what we are in design."

I think that Grandma Lamb really shows us what he means. How can she smile and be joyful when she never knows when the pain or weakness will go—or come again? She struggles to be herself, the way she was designed, right?!

I think that maybe God also struggles—and so really understands our pain, our fears.

Isabella, your Dad recently told me about your visit to a Disneyland princess store. The store featured those "magic eight balls"

---

[1] William Thomas, *What Are Old People For?: How Elders Will Save the World* (Vanderwyk & Burnham, 2004).

that you shake with the promise that you will receive an answer to any question. Dad assumed you would ask something like, "What princess will I be when I grow up?" But he was startled to hear you ask, "Why does God kill people?" The answer came back, "Try again. Ask a different question!" Disneyland was no help.

My "circle friends" here sometimes exchange ideas about that very important question. One is that while bad things too often happen, God only encourages us to do good things. That's why real heroes are special: they do good things even if they will be embarrassed, or hurt, or even killed. They want a better world. That's why your mothers endured pain so you would be born: you were God's idea inside them!

God loves us and the whole Cosmos so much, I think, that we are allowed to be good or bad. Countries sometimes attack other countries, people attack people. Terrible tsunamis kill innocent families and animals and trees. There is sometimes so much pain in our world! But, there is much, much more love—now and always and always.

Aren't so many of our days and years filled with hope and encouragement? Because there are so many good people, and friends, and fun pets, and monkey bars—and that incredible old sun always rises! There are Dr. Martin Luther Kings and Abraham Lincolns. Have you learned about Nelson Mandela or Dorothy Day yet? Who would you put on your lists of really good people? Special teachers and firefighters and artists and dancers?

Well, I especially thank God for YOU. And for creating a son, Jesus, to somehow always be with us. And also, so many people who work in our hospitals, speak other languages, and are badly paid, yet remain courageous and kind each and every day.

Love always,
Grandpa

#6

Hi Gabriel & Isabella!

I think this will be my last letter until Easter. Writing to you has given me much to think about. And I would like to first talk with you about some of our ideas and questions when we have time to sit together. Right now you are busy learning in school and everywhere.

Have you read any stories by Katherine Paterson who has written many children's stories? Let me know. I haven't yet but I have been reading about her. Like she wrote, "It is up to each of us not simply to write the words [of a story], but to be a word of hope made flesh."[1] I think she means that each of us—and our bodies are flesh, right—who cares about others, should act like good coaches and real friends.

Do you ever notice that sometimes we fail to encourage others? When you and I talk next, tell me if you agree people need to remind each other that God put inside each of us an idea to discover. An idea about how great each person can be.

TV advertisers are sometimes very clever. Have you seen how some are now telling athletes like soccer players and runners and gymnasts, "Buy our equipment for being what you were born to be." Special sneakers may sometimes help but I think the most important "equipment" has already been placed in our hearts and our minds.

For example, that's why on Fridays friends and I stand at the Four Corners here in Claremont. You have stood there, Isabella, and Gabriel when you were here last, you helped me put away all the yellow signs. We believe that war and hurting people to solve disagreements is bad. Bad because it blocks everyone's journey and search for that great idea God put in all of us!

And so I keep asking myself, "How can I be a better peacemaker, a word of hope made flesh? How can I be a better Elder-in-the-Making as well as an old person? If I believe, as I do, that everyone is created a child of God, why can't I try to make every person I meet feel welcomed?"

When Grandma and I left our work in Mexico to come home, I left behind a good friend and his family. Tomás Diaz is a potter, as was his father and his grandfather before him. He could never go to school but his grandmother taught him to read and write, and he came to value books as well as strangers as teachers.

I would sometimes visit him alone, or go early in the morning to drink *café con leche* with the whole family. Other days Grandma and I would take groups of seminary students and professors to talk with him. We would sit in a circle on the logs or big rocks outside his very simple house. Everyone was amazed by his wisdom and his questions—and inspired by his love of learning. Neighbors would come to Don Tomás

---

[1] Katherine Paterson, "Are You There God?" (*Harvard Divinity Bulletin*, Spring 2005).

for advice when there were problems. Sometimes mean political leaders promised to hurt him because he led his community in peaceful protests to demand justice for the Poor.

I tell you about Don Tomás because I think he is an ideal Elder. I have wanted to become more like him. Because old people, like young people, are different, of course there can be different kinds of Elders. But I think we old people can all share our knowledge and long experience. We can all try to listen carefully. We can speak the truth, become as "little children." We can strive to be "words of hope made flesh," meaning we can use our minds and bodies to encourage the discouraged to think well of themselves. And, to believe that together we can make a better world.

When I later write again, I want to tell you about a wonderful poet, a wonderful Elder who once lived at Pilgrim place. His name is Davie Napier. He is precious to all of us here because he was a good friend to all, a peace warrior, a grandfather of great strength and gentleness. Like Paulo and Don Tomás, he made both friends and strangers feel welcomed. Like them he was a Man of Hope.

And you well know there are many Women of Hope to talk about. When we do, I would like to include Joy Napier (Davie's wife); a fantastic Irish lady known as "Mother Jones"; and my grandmother, Daisy McDonnell, who was born in the Panama Canal Zone. You know where the Panama Canal is, right?

Gabriel and Isabella, because of who you are, you encourage me to be a Man of Hope. In fact, you make me think of one of the most beautiful words in our language: magnanimous. It has to be a large word because it means great-hearted, that is, very, very, very generous. Isabella, when your Mom & Dad return from Italy, ask them to say it in Italian. (In Spanish people sometimes say, ¡Dios es magnanimo!)

Well, my friends, I have talked too much. If you have a few free moments, or if you see opportunities at school, write to me. I promise to write back. But I especially look forward to talking, face to face, smile to smile—even tears to tears—whenever we are able.

I keep thinking about Lake Tahoe and One Who Trusts Others. How did our little duck friend learn to trust his/her own judgment about people and places? We may want to talk about that thought, and also the idea that the God who loves us so much, gave us the ability to become ALL that we already are. If we pay attention. If we bump into God as much as we can. If we stay excited. If we are sometimes willing to risk ourselves. If we keep loving and loving and loving—during our journeys.

> Big hugs from us here—Grandma doesn't know
> how to give little hugs, right?! Grandpa

Music, Ministry, Mystery

Barbara B. Troxell

April 2, 2008

INTRODUCTION

1. In the beginning was "Jesus loves me, This I know, for the Bible tells me so" and "Praise God, Praise God, all you little children, God is love, God is love." **In the beginning music was central to my perceiving the gracious love of God and of those around me.**

2. In my teen years, "O Jesus, I have promised to serve you to the end" and "A charge to keep I have, a God to glorify," led me to sensing a call to ordained pastoral ministry. **This call led to the challenge of claiming my God-given authority as a woman in ministry, and as a person ever growing and evolving in solidarity with others.**

3. Later there arose awareness of "Be still, and know that God is God . . ." and "Let all mortal flesh keep silence, and with fear and trembling stand . . ."[1] **The *honoring of the Mystery* at the heart of life led to more silence, more discernment, and more questions.**

So **Music, Ministry, Mystery** are the themes of my "doing theology." They are distinct, yet not separate. They intertwine and cycle around in every stage of my seventy-two years. For clarity in this presentation, I will take them in order, with awareness that they are cyclical and wondrously interrelated.

1. MUSIC

"Praise God, Praise God, all you little children, God is love, God is love!"

My father was a high school music teacher and minister of music at our local Methodist Church. From birth I was gifted with music all around me. Mother, Dad, sister Sally, and I loved singing in the church

---

[1] All lines from hymn texts, except "Praise God, praise God" and "Be still, and know," are in *The United Methodist Hymnal* (The United Methodist Publishing House, 1989), in public domain.

choirs, singing at home around the baby grand piano, listening to music on the radio and occasionally in concert halls. I also enjoyed playing rhythm instruments in kindergarten and later learning to play the piano. Music sang within me, played upon my being, and sent me on a continuing quest of moving more deeply into God and self, others and world.

Sometimes music even led me into Mystery, that which I could not comprehend with my mind but only with my wordless heart. But mostly, music fed me in grace-filled relationships: with family and friends at home, with choir members in local congregations, with college friends in Christian Association, with seminary friends in chapel services, with parishioners and colleagues in each of the congregations where I served as pastor, with pastors and friends in churches where I worshiped when I was in ministry beyond the local church, and now, in retirement, with Pilgrims in our Chorale and friends at Claremont United Methodist Church.

But I am getting ahead of myself. I grew up in Kings Highway Methodist Church, in Brooklyn, New York, a child-friendly congregation which was open to all sorts of people, though most of us in my childhood were white Euro-American Protestants. Thankfully, that church has continued to be reflective of its neighborhood, which now is primarily Afro-Caribbean. Kings Highway United Methodist Church also became a Reconciling Congregation (open and welcoming to gay and lesbian persons) several years ago. In my childhood and youth, there was real appreciation and affirmation of the gifts and skills of girls and women. We spent many hours a week at church: choir rehearsal for children and basketball practice happened Saturday mornings, basketball games were played Saturday nights and Wednesday nights, church school and worship on Sunday mornings, and in teen years Methodist Youth Fellowship Sunday nights.

I was a "good girl," an obedient child, often living out of other people's expectations. Mom and Dad were caring and affectionate parents, but did not teach me much about how to risk; I certainly did not "color outside the lines." Though I felt a nudging toward parish ministry as a teen-ager, the church vocations films shown at Methodist Youth Fellowship pictured clean-cut young men. So "girls can't be ministers" was the message I received loud and clear!

At "the Highway," as our church was familiarly called, I heard little about sin and evil, but much about the love, grace, and compassion of God in Sunday school, in choir anthems, in basketball playing, in worship services, in Methodist Youth Fellowship. A friend in high school confronted me several times as to whether I really was "saved" and knew Jesus as personal Savior. That was a different take on the faith than what I was accustomed to hearing at "the Highway." Her approach bothered me. I talked with our pastor, Dr. Tremayne, about it. He was helpful in explaining to me a variety of ways of understanding "salvation" and "doing theology."

In making music and listening to music, I began to be aware of the importance of the rests, the silences between the notes, so necessary to the rhythm and the tunes. Music, with its rests that inform its melodies and harmonies, offered a universality that opened me further to the rhythms of silence and speech, contemplation and action, within my relationships with family and friends, teachers and pastors, authors and artists, and people in other parts of the world about whom I read but had not personally met. Indeed, as I grew, I came to know the effect of different types of music on our very physiology, as well as our emotions and spirits.

2. MINISTRY

"A charge to keep I have, a God to glorify."

I moved from warm, protective, God-is-love home, school, and church in Brooklyn to Swarthmore College, in Pennsylvania. There I learned better study habits needed in that challenging academic environment. And there I also came to deeper appreciation of Jesus the Christ who lived, taught, healed, and was killed for his prophetic witness against oppressive authorities, both religious and state.

Through friends in the Christian Association and at Swarthmore Methodist Church I began to learn more of the meaning of the crucifixion and resurrection. In my junior year, Al Carmines (of blessed memory) arrived as a freshman. A committed southern Methodist Christian, he offered his strong witness, playing gospel songs and talking plenty about Jesus. A hymn I knew well, "When I survey the wondrous cross on which the prince of glory died," came alive for me, especially the last stanza: "Were the whole realm of nature mine, That were an offering far too small; Love so amazing, so divine, Demands my soul, my life, my all."

I sensed a strong call to ordained ministry, especially while serving in the Summer Projects Program of the Vermont Church Council, teaching daily vacation church school, preaching in rural churches, and living in parishioners' homes during two summers during college years. Though all the pastors I had previously known were male, in those summers I was encouraged by Catherine Smith, a Baptist clergywoman who served rural churches and after-school religious education programs in northern Vermont.

Union Theological Seminary had been calling out to me, since 1953 when I had spent a remarkable weekend there for college women considering theological education.[1] Liturgical piety, solid learning, and social justice came together in this ecumenical seminary in the heart of New York City, and in field education sites—one for a year in the Bronx, and the other for two years at Queens Village near Jamaica, Long Island. What learnings, what integrating of diverse God images occurred for me at Union! I was, however, unaware of the problem with masculine language and all-male pronouns until well after seminary. In fact in 1959 I wrote a B.D. (now M.Div.) dissertation on the church's ministry of healing, in New Testament and in contemporary settings, with much "man" and "he" language in it both for humans and for God! How could I! But that's what I knew in the 1950s.

After Union I took a year of postgraduate study at New College, Edinburgh, and was immersed in a felicitous combination of Scottish Christianity, John Wesley, and Karl Barth. Celtic Christianity's emphases on the sacredness of all of earth's creatures connected for me with, yet led me beyond, the summers at our Vermont lake cabin. The teaching and preaching of Professor James Stewart, of blessed memory, inspired me afresh with the way God's grace leads, guides, and calls. A group of Methodist students gathered once a week at the local Methodist church to study Wesley's sermons as we sipped tea and shared how the sermons impacted our lives. And Barth's neo-orthodoxy (as declaimed by Professor Thomas Torrance) made me dig more deeply into the meaning of Jesus Christ in my own life. In the spring of that year a life-changing pilgrimage to the Middle East, led by a British Methodist minister who had been a military chaplain there during World War II, brought vivid awareness of the oppression of Palestinians by the Israeli government, the evils of empire and colonialism, and the difficulty of resolving and reconciling conflicting claims.

In 1960, after returning from Scotland, I was appointed solo

---

[1] At that weekend for college women, I actually met Dr. Mary Ely Lyman, professor of Bible, and grandmother of Gene Boutilier. Wonder of wonders, that some fifty years later I would fall in love with her grandson here at Pilgrim Place, and marry him a couple of years later! God does work in wondrous ways.

pastor of Community Methodist Church in Cold Spring Harbor, New York, on the north shore of Long Island. In that small parish I loved the pastoral and liturgical responsibilities. The congregation received me well, as I listened carefully to their joys and struggles. I did "take authority" when I was preaching, leading liturgy, and praying with people in pastoral calling. In 1962 I even preached a sermon in which I urged parishioners to oppose fallout shelters and nuclear testing, and to support disarmament negotiations. This hit the local Long Island newspaper. But in organizational and administrative aspects, I depended on the laity and on "authorities" over me whom I considered greater or wiser than I. When it came to committee meetings and administrative roles, I tended to abdicate, for to take authoritative leadership seemed in some way "undemocratic" or not collegial enough with the laity.

Within my third year in the parish, having gone through an engagement and the breaking of the engagement with a man who was at Yale Divinity School, I began to discover myself more as a woman. I knew I needed to move into a form of ministry more conducive to exploring the feminine in me, in others, and in God. I felt the pressure of the "fish bowl"—that is, having to live my personal life in ways ever visible to the community within the small town around the church.

I struggled with what it means to be both woman and pastor, finally deciding to move into campus ministry, through the student YWCA. An important life-move, this decision took me first to Ohio, for three years as associate chaplain and YWCA director within Methodist-related Ohio Wesleyan University, and then to northern California for four remarkable years at Stanford. I flourished as I worked with young women and men in the upheavals of the 1960s. I grew in my understanding of justice issues: civil rights, racism, sexism, poverty, heterosexism, war and peace, especially during the time of the Vietnam war. I note today, regrettably, that sustainability and environmental justice were not much on our agenda.

At both Ohio Wesleyan and Stanford the issues of authority and mutual ministry became more dominant as crucial concerns for me, undergirded by an increasingly vital inner life and challenged by societal issues of justice and peace. I have high appreciation for the YWCA and that organization's strong commitment on behalf of women and against racism in all of its oppressive facets. I remember well the 1970 National Convention of the YWCA when the "One Imperative" was adopted, towards the "elimination of racism, wherever it exists and by any means necessary." During these years, in addition to some older sages, peers, and younger women of the YWCA, my mentors included Nelle Morton, Anne Bennett, Joy and Davie Napier, and Sydney and Robert McAfee Brown.[1]

I began to realize how strong was the patriarchy in the church and the society. I began to recognize how terrible was the discrimination against women—even against me many years before as a young candidate for ordained ministry. I remembered a meeting with an ordination board, when a totally male group of interviewers asked me no questions about theology, Bible, or my call. They asked: "Well, what if you get married? What if you have children? How will you pastor then?" For a woman who was a candidate for ordained ministry, those kinds of questions clearly were discriminatory.

The summer of 1963, soon after I arrived at Ohio Wesleyan, I was introduced to the Grail Movement at the national center, Grailville. That's where I first met Donna Myers (Ambrogi), Eva Fleischner, and Audrey Sorrento. The Grail was a movement of progressive Catholic women who combined a solid sense of worship, a deep understanding of the strong roles of women, and work for justice and reconciliation throughout the world. By the late 60s several of us Protestant women joined the Grail. In the early 1970s one of the first ecumenical "women doing theology" conferences was hospitably hosted at Grailville.

During a sabbatical in 1970-71 I met women at Pacific School of Religion who were astute feminists. I read Rosemary Ruether, Elizabeth Schussler Fiorenza, Letty Russell, Mary Daly, and other feminist theologians. Entering a team ministry in 1971 at First Presbyterian Church of Palo Alto led me to deeper appropriation of a feminist and anti-racist agenda.

Together with a sensitive and wise male senior pastor, other staff, and superb laity, we made inclusive our worship language about God. I remember the Sunday when I dared to give a benediction which included "our Mother-Father God"! That was received well by many parishioners, yet caused quite a negative stir for others; significant conversations followed. I preached every other Sunday, led women's study groups, and was fully involved in parish life. First Pres. held together well the vitality of worship and the prophetic witness, including

---

[1] Some of the stories told in *Journeys That Opened Up the World*, edited by Sara M. Evans (Rutgers University Press, 2003), which book honors Ruth Harris, and has chapters by Ruth, Eleanor Scott Meyers, Jeanne Audrey Powers, and other friends, connect vividly with my story as staff with the Student YWCA.

becoming a sanctuary church for a soldier resisting the Vietnam War.[1]

Seminars on "The Life and Teachings of Jesus," sponsored by The Guild for Psychological Studies and led by wise guides who honored both the holistic presence of Jesus in the synoptic gospels and the insights of Jungian depth psychology, aided me considerably in my own quest. Intensive biblical study on the authority of Jesus helped me deepen my understanding of the differences between legitimated authority (*exousia*) and raw power (*dunamis*).[2] Later, therapy with an insightful Jungian analyst, one of the founders of the Guild, was enormously motivating toward claiming my own inner God-given authority. When my mother died, too young, quite close to my fortieth birthday, the studies with the Guild, the Jungian analysis, and the community of First Presbyterian Church all assisted me in coming to a sense of the inner motherhood of God. When my biological mother was no longer available in the flesh, the inner Mother God emerged.

In the 1970s, I was a member of the board of The General Commission on the Status and Role of Women of The United Methodist Church, whose mission was (and still is) to be advocate, catalyst, and monitor for women in the denomination. In the parish, in the YWCA, in the Commission on the Status and Role of Women, in the Guild, and in Jungian analysis, I began to appropriate more of my own inner authority and inner wisdom, which related deeply to the feminine Divine. I came in touch with fresh voices who called me to honor the wisdom within, the insight and intuition which is borne in our own lively woman souls.

In 1978 Bishop Marvin Stuart, of the California Nevada Conference, appointed me a District Superintendent. By the second year of the superintendency, I entered spiritual direction for the first time. I felt the need for a pastoral presence with me, someone I could trust to help me tend my own soul, someone who would support and hold me accountable in my journey with God.[3] I found a wise younger woman

---

[1] See my chapter, "Team Ministry as Possibility," in *Women in a Strange Land,* edited by Anne Bennett and Clare Fischer (Fortress Press, 1975).

[2] I engaged in a personal study of the synoptic passages where the authority of Jesus is questioned and affirmed, such as Mark 1:22, 27, 2:10, 11:28.

[3] It is difficult to be tending of one's own soul when one is a United Methodist district superintendent, for the superintendent is to be both pastor to and supervisor of pastors and congregations. Some of us were led (I was and am glad about it) to emphasize the pastoral; others were on the side of being highly supervisorial and authoritarian.

who had had solid training both as a spiritual director and as a therapist and knew the difference between those two callings. I continued with Pam as long as I lived in the Bay Area. And I have continued in spiritual direction monthly in every location where I have lived since.

Though I was claiming more of my own authority in God, and was living more fully out of that conviction, I continued to struggle with the tension of outer expectations versus inner witness. This process was focused, during the period 1975-84, in discerning whether I should let my name be put forth as a candidate for the United Methodist episcopacy. Prior to each of three quadrennial meetings, Jurisdictional Conferences where bishops are elected, colleagues and friends whose judgment I respected and valued felt that I would be an excellent bishop. In the late 70s some wanted me to be a pioneer, the first woman bishop within the denomination. I explored this opportunity, prayed much about it, and consulted with trusted friends.

I knew I could do the work, had the gifts for the office, and would be a good bishop. However, the inner witness kept coming up negative, that somehow this was not the will of God for me at that time in my life. In the discernment, there was also the matter of having a personal life, desiring a life-companion, and knowing that such a process would be much harder to pursue and follow, were I to be elected bishop. So I said a clear "No" each time.

Was I abdicating? Perhaps there was some fear of risk-taking. But more so, there was a sense that my inner authority (the "inner witness" of the Spirit, as John Wesley would term it) was not affirming the move to a role and an office where outer authority would be visibly and powerfully evident. My soul needed more tending. My personal life needed more honoring. So the decision was made, each time in 1976, 1980, and 1984—that becoming bishop was not the call of God for me.

After a welcome sabbatical study year following the superintending term, I was invited in 1984 to become Dean of Students at Pacific School of Religion. My position description included major emphases on spiritual formation, seminary worship life, and community-building with students and faculty. We faced the new crisis of HIV and AIDS with some male seminarians. We looked squarely at the discrimination in the church against gay and lesbian persons. I affirmed again and again the presence of the Holy One who creates all of us as "good," and as made in the image of God.

In 1988, after a year as an associate pastor in Oakland focusing on spiritual formation, I made a major life-move from California to Chicago, with my then-husband, for his work. Within a few months I was invited to be on the faculty at Garrett-Evangelical Theological Seminary, a United Methodist seminary, in Evanston, Illinois. I was director of field education, taught courses in spiritual formation, and later also co-taught United Methodist studies. The years at Garrett-Evangelical called forth the best of where I had been in ministry, and drew me further forward and more deeply inward. The questions and concerns around authority continued to prod and nudge me to fuller life in God and in God's world. I worked with students to help them claim their authority in God, while encouraging mutual ministry. I interviewed women in positions of authority in The United Methodist Church in order to write a chapter for a book on women in the United Methodist tradition.[1]

Through the years I have learned much about facing conflict. Though I came from a family and an early educational system that prized order and suppression of disagreement, I have seen the great value of the tension engendered by conflict. I understand the transforming power of creativity and change that occurs only in places of chaos and upheaval. For example, my eyes and ears and heart have been opened to the pain and the potential of outstanding and faithful clergywomen and men who have found the church's limiting boundaries, such as the prohibitive language against lesbians and gays, too restrictive for their God-given gifts, calling, and identity. Their challenges provoke the church and all of us to necessary change. As a pacifist who holds decades-long memberships in both the Methodist Federation for Social Action (MFSA) and the Fellowship of Reconciliation (FOR), I have learned to take initiative to confront and transform conflicts for the well-being of all. Yet so much more is needed.

I remember the first Re-Imagining Conference of 1993. As each plenary presenter was escorted to the center stage, we were invited to stretch out our arms (all 2300 of us!) and sing this blessing: "Bless Sophia, dream the vision, share the wisdom dwelling deep within."

I was excited and encouraged by the Re-Imagining Conference (and its successor conferences) where the feminine Divine moved deeply and creatively within me and around me. Immediately after the event,

---

[1] "Honoring One Another With Our Stories," my chapter in *Spirituality and Social Responsibility: Vocational Vision of Women in The United Methodist Tradition*, Rosemary Skinner Keller, editor (Abingdon Press, 1993).

enormous backlash erupted from conservative caucuses of several denominations. They believed that to "re-imagine" God, Christ, church, work, marriage and family, was to be heretical. They believed that offering a "Sophia blessing" was blasphemous, for they saw Sophia as a goddess in competition with the true God—rather than as a feminine aspect (or companion) of the Divine Holy One.

Now in my eighth decade, I honor that holy Wisdom, that Sophia aspect of God, even more strongly and deeply. She is not to be ignored. She is Guide and Wise Companion.

3. MYSTERY

"Let all mortal flesh keep silence, and with fear and trembling stand."

How do I experience the sacred, the mystery at the heart of the universe, the presence of the living God now? Music continues to sing in and through me, and lead me more deeply into the Holy One. Ministry continues in various forms, as I offer spiritual guidance to individuals and as I lead workshops and retreats. Streams of spirituality within the tradition of the church and within my own experience continue to flow and inform who I am. I continue to be grateful for spiritual direction about once a month.[1]

Within Mystery are some significant affirmations and wonderings:

Embodiment: God is incarnate not only in the flesh of Jesus but in our flesh, our bodies. We, all of us, are bearers of the holy. The Divine is incarnate in us. With Mary, each of us is *theotokos*, a God-bearer.

Relational connectedness: The sacred mystery of God dwells not only in me[2] and in other humans but in the interconnectedness of us with one another and with other creatures in all times and places (plants,

---

[1] As someone recently said, therapy concludes when one can cope better and feels healed; spiritual direction is life-long, for one is ever growing in the journey with God. In addition to being in spiritual direction myself, I learned much of the contemplative way from the two-year Spiritual Guidance Program of The Shalem Institute.

[2] And as 2 Timothy 1:5 states, "in your grandmother . . . and your mother"—my middle name is Bea, a short form of my mother's and maternal grandmother's name, Beatrix.

trees, birds, rocks, animals, reptiles, insects) all created by a God who is ultimately relational and interactive with all of creation. This quality of relational connectedness includes the gift of our sexuality—how we express and live out who we are as sexual beings who love and are loved. Connectedness includes a sense of the sacred in all of creation, a sacramental attentiveness to and connectivity with all that is.

Mutuality within interdependence: Most women desire and prefer mutuality, rather than hierarchy. We seek the wisdom of others on many levels, not only the perspective of "experts." We learn to trust our own inner God-given wisdom. We usually prefer collaboration rather than competition, mutuality rather than rampant individualism.

Hearing one another into speech: This is Nelle Morton's felicitous phrase, as she tells the story of a woman in a 1971 consciousness-raising group who did not readily speak. When the woman began to talk and weep, no one interrupted her or cut her short. The woman ended by saying: "You heard me. You heard me all the way . . . I have a strange feeling you heard me before I started. You heard me to my own story. You heard me to my own speech." Nelle Morton offers enormous insight that has aided us in our attentiveness and deep listening: no interruption, no rush to comfort, no cutting short of another's experience; but sitting "in a powerful silence," going with the weeping one to "the deepest part of her life as if something so sacred was taking place they did not withdraw their presence or mar its visibility."[1]

Prayer in many forms:

Prayer of silent attentiveness to what is, of "mindfulness" through the day;

Prayer of appreciation of beauty in creation and in human life, even in places of sadness, shadow, poverty;

Prayers from some Psalms: of lament, of protest, of struggle;

Prayer in music: in listening, in playing, in singing;

Prayer through our bodies: moving, dancing, bowing, stretching;

Prayers of intercession: on behalf of other people and our world;

Prayer both alone and with others: I am most able to enter into contemplative silence when I am with people who support my attentiveness and hold me accountable to it; and corporate, sacramental worship is central to my faith.

---

[1] Nelle Morton, *The Journey Is Home* (Beacon Press, 1985), 204-205.

Necessary questions: Within the Mystery are large periods of silence, pauses, musical rests that are essential to the fullness of the Holy in our midst. Within the Mystery are laments and agonizing questions about the brokenness and violence within this world.

> Why, O God, when you desire our well-being is there such terrible pain? Why do we humans inflict excruciating violence on one another and on our earth? What ails us, and whom do we serve?[1] How can we collaborate with you, gracious God, in the saving of this planet? How can peace and reconciliation and healing grow? How can we be trusting and joyful and full of hope, when there is so much agony?

With the continuing questions, somehow, within Mystery are flashes of joy, amazing alleluias, and songs without words that keep on flowing.

So how can we keep from singing?

CONCLUSION

Lately I have been returning to the beginnings—awareness of the power of music and relationships throughout my life; appreciation for a remarkable forty-plus years of active ministry in which inner and outer authority jostled me, disturbed me, and often came together in wondrous ways; gratitude for the church as community of faith and promise, yet with so much ambiguity;[2] the gift of fast-moving retirement years in this beloved community that supports and challenges and prods me to remember.

God images grounded in the musical and loving beginnings have evolved into less absolutes and more questions, openness, and wildness:

God as loving Father/Mother;

God in Jesus Christ, all that Jesus evokes in his life, teachings, healings, death at hands of evil powers, resurrection, and in beginning communities of the Way;

God as Spirit, who is "Love that wilt not let me go";

---

[1] In the Grail legend, these are the questions asked of the Fisher King when Parsifal is searching for the Grail. The Grail Movement of women also includes these two questions in our tradition, as we emphasize a concern for others in need.

[2] I love the Church and its sacramental life. Into it I was born, within it I have been nurtured and led, with it I have had many lover's quarrels. Now I find myself not wanting to spend time and energy on institutional church struggles, while at the same time knowing that this fragile, sinful human community is called to work with God towards the salvation of the world.

God as inclusive of feminine qualities as well as masculine;
God always on the side of the poor and marginalized;
God not only as Parent, but as Lover;
God as Companion with us, Challenger to us, and Mystery beyond
us;
Trinity as God ever-Creator, ever-Emmanuel, ever-transforming
Spirit;
Trinity as "Life-Giver, Pain-bearer, Love-Maker." (Jim Cotter)[1]

God, Holy One, more than any of these!

And ultimately pregnant silence, where I am "lost in wonder, love, and praise."[2]

---

[1] I first learned of Jim Cotter's trinitarian phrase in one of his versions of the Prayer of Jesus, in *Prayer at Night's Approaching* (Cairns Publications, 1997).

[2] Last line of Charles Wesley's fine hymn, "Love divine, all loves excelling." The Wesley hymns have been a sustaining aspect of my faith.

Looking Death in the Face
Charles Bayer
April 16, 2008

This monograph is about death. It will eventually focus on the death of my son, John, but it is also about all deaths, particularly my own. Two years ago, when I wrote my memoirs for family members, Wendy suggested that although I had gotten most of the facts straight, I had included little of the deeper places in my life. In this essay I will try to do some of that unfinished work. I will not reveal everything. In fact there are things about my inner life I do not even know. If the adage, "know yourself" is an axiom of good living, it is also really hard work. How can anyone know what goes on under the surface? I'll get back to that in a bit. "Who am I?" asked Bonhoeffer from his prison cell. Oscar Wilde is reported to have said, "Be yourself. Everyone else is already taken." Nevertheless, I have never really known what it means to be myself. I will get to John's death, but first I have some wandering around to do—so be patient.

In 1966 I was securely rooted in a solid suburban church with a pleasant parsonage and a typical nuclear family. Of the three children, the youngest, John, was age 6. I was President of the Washington, D.C. Area Council of Churches, and life was uncomplicated. And then I got a call to become pastor of a congregation on the campus of the University of Chicago. It was, and still is, the liberal bellwether of our denomination.

Among the problems in moving to Chicago's South Side was putting our previously sheltered children in the toughest public schools anywhere. But church people said that was no issue. By the time we arrived, they weren't so sure, and suggested that we enroll the children in John Dewey's Lab School. But the fee was six thousand dollars a pop, and eighteen thousand was well over half of my total salary. But I believed in pubic education, and have often wondered about liberals whose children are in private—safer—schools.

When I arrived on the South side of Chicago, the great Dutch gothic church building was locked tight except Sunday mornings for an hour and another hour Thursday evenings for choir practice. Part of my condition for coming was to be allowed to unlock the door and spend a significant portion of the endowment. The moment the key was turned in the lock we were inundated by students. It was the high point of the anti-Vietnam war movement, and we quickly became the center for the radical students—thousands of them. We probably had 500 people in the building every day. I became their pastor, was gassed at Michigan and Balboa during the 1968 Democratic Convention, and was called as a suspected conspirator by the Grand Jury that led to the trial of the Chicago 8. But that is another story. We also became the safe house for the two rival Black street gangs in Chicago—the Devil's Disciples and the Blackstone Rangers. But that is still another story.

The upshot was that my focus was taken off my family and immersed in this 20-hour-a-day caldron. Our elder daughter left home at 17 without support and with no high school diploma. Two years later, with no parental help, nor any money, she was mysteriously enrolled in an elegant woman's College in Norton, Massachusetts. Another story yet. She eventually became an outstanding psychiatrist, and today lives on a yacht at Catalina Island.

The younger daughter, after getting involved in God knows what, ended up in Wisconsin, finally became a graduate nurse and now runs a hospice in New Orleans. Despite what they experienced in Hyde Park, they both landed on their feet—little thanks to me. Both daughters are now devotedly close to Wendy and to me.

John, however, barely survived. Not surprisingly, the family disintegrated. I guess I was dimly aware of it. The result was a divorce and I left University Church to become Executive Director of a not-for-profit corporation in the Loop. John, age 13, tired of the fight over his future, hired his own lawyer, and I was awarded custody. So John and I lived together. How was I going to handle that? I was totally unequipped. I had been a consultant to a high school that sent kids on a year's educational voyage aboard a three-mast schooner, and John went to sea. He came back and entered Evanston High School where his moxie got him through until he and I moved to St. Joseph where I reentered the pastoral ministry. The two of us survived an often tense relationship.

A year later Wendy and her three children entered our lives, and we were married in a Sunday morning worship service. Order was at last brought to this chaos. It was Wendy who saved my sanity. The blended family worked well, with John still suffering from the scars endured in Chicago.

After high school John attended a merchant marine academy and became a mate on a ship carrying liquid natural gas around the world. He would come home for a quick visit every year or so, bouncing in loaded with trinkets. The little kids of the family called him Tigger, and he called them the munchkins.

In February 1985 he was on his way to Missouri, and had stopped off in Florida where he and a couple of cousins rented an airplane for a surfboarding trip up the coast. Late Saturday evening I got a call from my younger daughter telling me that the plane had crashed and all three had been killed.

Wendy says I wailed, but I have no recollection. I knew I had to get to Florida and said I would do it after I handled the Sunday morning services. Wendy knew better and called our Associate, Wally Reed, who came to the house where he and Wendy made the decision I was too unraveled to make.

I arrived in Florida, went to the little airport, and was taken to the charred remains of the plane. There were no bodies, only ashes. There was not enough left of John's body to be viewed. My younger daughter came from New Orleans, and we had a memorial service at the church in Ft. Myers. My father, who could never deal with anything unpleasant, lived in the community, but a "cold in the head" kept him from the funeral. When his only other son, my brother, was dying and began to cry as our father entered his hospital room, Dad said, "Peter, we don't do that in our family." But that is still another story. My younger daughter and Wendy and I then met in New Orleans where my elder daughter was about to give birth. She did in a few days, and the child was named John.

We returned to St. Joseph where the community held a memorial service attended by several hundred and hosted at the church by a funeral director as a gift to me.

I might admire those who breeze through grief or at least seem able quickly to look beyond it. They are often called people of great faith. I am not in that number. For the next eight weeks I did not get through a morning worship service without coming apart. The congregation, the church staff and Wendy took care of me.

I conducted 600 funerals while at that church; half from the congregation and half from the community, where I was public figure. I had known that every Sunday when I stood in that pulpit I looked out over a sea of broken hearts, and now my heart had been shattered. Throughout my ministry there I had ended the worship service at least once a month by saying, "Be very kind to one another, for most of us are fighting a hard battle." Now that truth became "up-close and personal."

John was dead. He had not gone over, passed away, moved to a better place, was safe in heaven, or had slipped off this mortal coil. He had died, and it was final. I did not sleep. I did not eat. I did not function for weeks. And then one night I had a dream. Wendy and I were in a big auditorium, perhaps at the high school. On stage was our church choir with Richard, our choir director. He had written a song—real tuneful music—which the choir sang. It was called, "John is back." Then from the side of the stage John appeared. Without words he said to me, "I'm not back. I don't want to be back. Get on with it." That dream broke open my grief, and I was able to pick life up again.

From that day until this John has resided out of sight, just in back of my right shoulder, and occasionally without warning will dart in front of me. For a moment the grief rushes back. But these days it is gentler and evokes pleasant memories of that little fellow sitting patiently in a chair, while I ran clippers over his head.

I did other things to deal with my grief. Wendy and I bought a fisherman's cabin on the coast of Maine, where we spent summers, thanks to a generous vacation and study policy by the congregation. I learned to sail and purchased a 24-foot sloop, which we called THE JOHN MARK. I took flying lessons and became an instrument-rated pilot. If children often follow in their father's footsteps, I followed in John's.

Since that time more than a quarter of a century ago, I have maintained an aggressive schedule. I have retired three times and still operate a sturdy work discipline. Friends—some at Pilgrim Place—have suggested that I ease up, admit my age and relax. But I feel relaxed in what I do.

Who knows why many of us here keep going as if we were half our age? After all, we are either approaching or beyond our use-by date. In the US, life expectancy for women is 80.4 and for men 75.2. If we make it to 60 those figures go up. For women: 82.4 and for men 78.2. When someone at Pilgrim Place dies I will say to Wendy, "We have just moved up in the queue."

If I were in therapy, perhaps it would be suggested that my drive might come from an effort to fight off death. When the sands are running out in one's hourglass, perhaps for some of us there is an obsession to complete an agenda. Or what is seen as our drivenness may flow from guilt, related to something very different we had neglected. Could that be true in my case?

Who knows? Sidney Lanier reflected on the marshes of Glynn off the Georgia coast. When the tides come in and the marshes are flooded, all one sees is the calm surface. But what is underneath?

And now from the Vast of the Lord will the waters of sleep
Roll in on the souls of men,
But who will reveal to our waking ken
The forms that swim and the shapes that creep
       Under the waters of sleep?
And I would I could know what swimmeth below when the tide
    comes in
On the length and the breadth of the marvelous marshes of Glynn.

It may be the threat of death. It may be some guilt. I do not know, and I really do not care. What I do know is that

. . . I have promises to keep,
And miles to go before I sleep,
And miles to go before I sleep.[1]

So what out of my experience do I make of death? I know that deep at the heart of Christianity is the story of the resurrection and the promise of eternal life. I can recite 1 Corinthians 15 as well as anyone. I have stood with hundreds of families who knew that their loved ones were safe up there somewhere beyond the sunset, and that they would all be joined again in the sweet by-and-by, when they would rest on that beautiful shore.

I guess there are moments I would like to believe that, but I remain an agnostic. I tend to see the resurrection and the eternal life of our biblical passages as relating to hope for the world, for God's gracious care for all of us, and not as an individual guarantee that I'll get up there someday. I know that from the dust I came and to it I will return—as quickly as a fire will accomplish it. And I know of my life, that the wind will pass over it, and it will be remembered no more.

When I was a child, even if I believed all the orthodox things, I still occasionally shook with fright at the notion that someday I would cease to be. The older I get and the closer to the edge of that reality, the less death bothers me, if death means oblivion. I don't know if there is any personal survival beyond this life. I am perfectly willing to leave that to my Creator.

Perhaps each of us is given a tiny trifling bit of space and a smidgeon of time in which to live, and while what we do with it does not determine how we shall come out at death, it may influence how this life

---

[1] Robert Frost, "Stopping by Woods on a Snowy Evening."

will be better for a few others trying to make it in an often hard world.

Shakespeare might have been half right. An individual's life may be like *"a poor player / That struts and frets his hour upon the stage / And then is heard no more."* But it is not simply *"a tale / Told by an idiot, full of sound and fury, / Signifying nothing."*[1] I do not know what lies in God's providence. But I try to be faithful to what the saint who was out plowing said when he was asked what he would do if he knew he would die that night. Looking down the field he replied, "I'd plow as straight a furrow this afternoon as I could."

Nor do I have an inclination to muse about those notions that assume we are part body and part soul, and that the latter goes on existing without the former. Speculation about reincarnation, which assumes that souls jump from one existence to another, finds me increasingly doubtful.

I had a little dog, and his name was Rover.
And when he died he died all over.[2]

For me the resurrection is God's testimony to new life, but that may not be focused on my personal existence in some other conscious form, but on the hope that is brought from death to life in every generation. When at funerals there is some great-grandbaby who begins to fuss and cry and a parent hurries to take them out, I always stop them and ask the congregation to listen to that cry, for *"a generation comes and a generation goes, but the word of our God endures forever."*

I've had a pretty good run at it, living almost twice as long already as the average resident who has inhabited this planet. John's run was not that good, and much of it was troubled.

How does one stand with the bereaved without giving in to a folklore, which may be comforting but which tends to deny the absolute worth of every minute and every breath right here and right now?

I end this essay with an ancient prayer I have uttered hundreds of times over the graves of somebody's mother, father, sister, brother, partner, daughter or son.

O Lord, support us all the day long of this troublous life,
Until the shadows lengthen and the evening comes,
And the busy world is hushed, and the fever of life is over

---

[1] *Macbeth*, Act V, scene 5.

[2] Attributed to Elsie Strawn Armstrong.

And our work is done.
Then of thy mercy, grant us a safe lodging,
And a holy rest, and peace at the last, through Jesus Christ, our
Lord.[1]

---

[1] Attributed to John Henry, Cardinal Newman.

Change
Richard Moore
May 7, 2008

To lead a life worthy of the Sovereign, fully pleasing to him,
being fruitful in every good work, and increasing
in the knowledge of God.
(A paraphrase of Colossians 1:10)

"There is no God external to life. God, rather, is the inescapable
depth and center of all that is.
God is not a being superior to all other beings.
God is the Ground of Being itself."
(John Shelby Spong, *Why Christianity Must Change or Die*, 70)

My earliest memories of church are of being dragged up the steps to the front door of the Presbyterian Church in Babylon, Long Island, New York, after having attended Sunday School. My parents served in various offices in the church and they thought that the worship experience would be beneficial for me and my sister. Prior to the sermon the children were dismissed to the classrooms where we played Bible Lotto.

     In 1940 we moved from Babylon to a five-acre hillside lot owned by my mother's father with apple trees, peach trees, and plenty of room for a garden, with a house built in the late 18th or early 19th century in Marion, Connecticut. We attended the Congregational Church in Plantsville where my parents again participated in leadership positions. In Sunday School we sang:

> *Who is on the Lord's side? Who will serve the King?*
> *Who will be his helpers, other lives to bring?*
> *Who will share the burden, Lighten toil and woe?*
> *Who will ask no guerdon but with him will go?*
> *By thy call of mercy, by thy grace divine,*
> *We are on the Lord's side, Saviour, we are thine.*[1]

At the expected time I joined the pastor's confirmation class and became a member of the church. My high school was Lewis High School in Southington, Connecticut.

---

[1] As in *The New Hymnal for American Youth* (Fleming H. Revell Company, 1930).

Both of my parents were natives of Connecticut, but they met in Massachusetts, where my mother was a student at Smith College (in spite of the fact that her father did not think that a woman needed a college education) and my father was a student at Springfield College. Their education was interrupted by their marriage at an Episcopal Church in Waterbury, Connecticut, and my birth months later. In 1944 as I was about to finish high school, and would soon be subject to the military draft, my father arranged for me to leave high school after three and a half years and enter Trinity College in Hartford, Connecticut, an Episcopal college for men, where I was able to complete my freshman year prior to being drafted. In spite of the fact that I had left high school early I had enough credits to graduate with my class as Salutatorian in June 1944.

Prior to being drafted I took a test called the Eddy Test which placed me in training as an electronic technician in the Navy. From Great Lakes Training Center I entered the classes in electronics at the Navy Pier in Chicago. I sang in the chorus at chapel services and thus was among those sent on liberty prior to lining up for inspection. Within the Loop in downtown Chicago I attended the Service Center sponsored by the Christian Businessmen. Here we met with other military personnel and were hosted by volunteers, one of whom sat me down and demanded to know if I was a Christian. I was surprised to learn that my Congregational church membership was not adequate if I could not state the exact date upon which I had been converted, repented of my sins, and accepted Jesus as my personal savior. So then and there I said the required words, and repeated my "personal testimony" to another one of the workers. This placed me on a series of "Gospel Teams" which visited various evening services at churches throughout the Chicago area. Sometimes we would hand out tracts en route, and on the train we sang loudly, *"This world is not my home; I'm just a-passing through; my treasures are laid up somewhere beyond the blue."* We also visited patients at Cook County Hospital with our so-called Gospel message of salvation.

The message was contained in the argument still being proclaimed by fundamentalist ministers as follows:

Realize there is none good (Romans 3:10).
See yourself as a sinner (Romans 3:23).
Recognize where sin came from (Romans 5:12).
Notice God's price on sin (Romans 6:23).
Realize that Christ died for you (Romans 5:8).

Repent of your sin (Acts 17:30).

Take God at God's word and claim God's promise for your salvation. (Romans 10:9-10,13; John 3:16).

After my training as an electronic technician I was transferred to California where, World War II having ended, I was assigned to help decommission troop ships in Stockton. With this background, when I was discharged from the Navy, feeling a call to Christian ministry, and seeking a "Christian" school, I chose to enter Houghton College, sponsored by the Wesleyan Methodist denomination in Houghton, New York. Upon admission I was granted college credit for military service with a minor in science. I chose to major in Greek and, although I did poorly in this language study, my instructor, knowing that I was a Greek major, granted me a C grade. Thus I was able to graduate from college in the year 1948, the same year as if I had gone into college directly from high school without taking time out for military service, much to the approval of my parents.

It was the practice of Houghton College to invite evangelists to campus for special services directed toward the spiritual development of students. On one of these occasions I had conversation with the guest minister, a Presbyterian, and I sought his guidance as to how I should seek ordination as an ordained minister. Should I change denominations? He asked me what I wanted to do, and I replied that I wanted to bring new life into the Congregational churches. His response was, "Then, do it!" I was not sure how I would do this, but somehow I anticipated leading people to a literal understanding of the Bible.

In the fall of 1948 I enrolled in Eastern Baptist Theological Seminary (now Palmer Theological Seminary) in Philadelphia. My experience in ministry began while I was in college when I served as assistant minister at a Methodist church in Dalton, New York, a church which was served by a part-time minister whose weekday employment was as a barber. Prior to my first year in seminary I served as a counselor at a summer camp on the shore of Lake Winnipesaukee in New Hampshire, and after my first year at seminary I served as summer student minister at three preaching points in Maine: Sunday River, North Newry, and Upton. Since students in seminary were required to do some church-related work I became the minister at Kensington Congregational Church in the Kensington section of Philadelphia. As a licensed minister of the Central Association of the Congregational Christian Churches, I was permitted to preach and preside at the sacraments.

Needing an organist and choir director, I enlisted the services of Grace Jones, who was studying for a Master of Religious Education degree. We became engaged in 1950 when Grace moved to become Director of Christian Education and Minister of Music at First Baptist Church in Keokuk, Iowa. Upon graduation from seminary in 1951, I was a member of the class not required to write a thesis, but to take a comprehensive examination instead. (We were not informed the results of this exam.) In April of 1951 I was ordained by the Central Association of Congregational Christian Churches at the Kensington Church, and after my graduation from seminary, Grace and I were married at Calvary Church in Placentia, California. This was the church attended by Grace's parents, a fundamentalist congregation which had been established by evangelist Charles E. Fuller, but was served by another minister when we were married. Our wedding rings were inscribed with the Bible reference Col. 1:10.[1] My parents flew back to Connecticut and Grace and I drove my parents' car to North Canaan, Connecticut where I had been called to serve the Pilgrim Congregational Church.

When I was installed as pastor in Canaan by the North Litchfield Association, I chose to read the same paper I had prepared for my ordination. In the question period I was asked what I would do if a Unitarian applied for church membership, and I replied that I would deny the request. The questioners were not pleased with this response, and when I left the room for their discussion period, as I learned later, they decided that if I were seeking ordination they would deny it, but since I was already ordained and had begun to minister in Canaan, they would install me.

While at Canaan I attended several summer retreats for Congregational ministers, and I was a delegate to the national General Council meeting of the Congregational Christian Churches held in Claremont, California in 1952. These experiences moved me away from my extreme conservatism toward a liberal theology.

In 1954 I resigned from the church in Canaan. We sold most of our furniture, packed our remaining possessions in a rental trailer and moved to California, where we stayed with Grace's parents at their orange grove in Villa Park. Receiving a call to the Community Congregational Church of San Ysidro under the sponsorship of the Southern California Conference and the Board of Home Missions, we

---

[1] See the top of the first page of this paper.

moved to what was once the "Little Landers Colony" at the southern tip of California bordering Tijuana, Mexico. Here there was a small group of faithful members who were joined by the families of employees of the Border Patrol. At the request of several persons who desired to become church members, I baptized them in the pool of a neighboring Baptist congregation in Chula Vista. This has been my only experience with baptism by immersion.

From San Ysidro we moved on to other parishes in Southern California, including my service as Assistant Minister at Kensington Community (Congregational) Church in San Diego, pastor of the First Congregational Church in Barstow, pastor of the West Garden Grove United Church of Christ, co-interim pastor at the Garden Grove UCC, Youth Minister with John and Peg Reynolds at the Neighborhood Congregational Church in Laguna Beach, and co-pastor with Grace at the Lakewood Community Church, UCC. We retired in 1991 and moved to Pilgrim Place in late December 2000.

I have participated in the life of the United Church of Christ at the Association and Conference levels, and served as a delegate to meetings of the General Synod a number of times. My theology has changed through the years with participation in several clergy groups, and a variety of pastoral conferences sponsored by the national United Church of Christ, the School of Theology at Claremont, and the Pacific School of Religion.

My ministry has been developed in partnership with my wife, Grace, organist, choir director, Christian educator and ecumenical and community leader. For a time Grace was employed as secretary for the Center for Metropolitan Mission and In-Service Training in Los Angeles, working with Paul Kittlaus and Speed Leas. Long active in the UCC Conference Women's Fellowship and Church Women United, she became an active participant in the Conference Women's Task Force which met frequently at our home and made a study of both Church School literature and corporate advertisements from a gender-inclusive and feminist perspective. Grace was ordained by the Central Association of the UCC on April 29, 1973. Following that, Grace spent several years commuting to Immaculate Heart College where she earned a Masters degree in Feminist Spirituality. Of course, all of this had an influence on my theology, attitudes and use of language in conversation and worship leadership.

A Concern for the Environment

"We have not inherited the Earth from our fathers,
we are borrowing it from our children."
(Native American Proverb)

God created great sea monsters and all sorts of swimming creatures
with which the waters are filled, and all kinds of birds. God saw that
this was good and blessed them saying, "Bear fruit, increase your
numbers, and fill the waters of the seas! Birds, abound on the earth!"
(Genesis 1:21-22, *The Inclusive Bible*)

"Humankind was created as God's reflection, in the divine image
God created them, female and male. God made them. God blessed
them and said, 'Bear fruit, increase your numbers, and fill the earth—
and be responsible for it! Watch over the fish of the sea, the birds of
the air, and all the living things on the earth!' God told them, 'Look,
I give you every seed-bearing plant on the face of the earth, and every
tree whose fruit carries its seed inside itself: they will be your food;
and to all the animals of the earth and the birds of the air and things
that crawl on the ground—everything that has a living soul in it—I
give all the green plants for food.' So it was."
(Genesis 2:27-30, *The Inclusive Bible*)

"Not all flesh is the same. Human beings have one kind, animals
have another, birds another and fish another. Then there are
heavenly bodies and earthly bodies. Heavenly bodies have a beauty
of their own, and earthly bodies have a beauty of the own."
(1 Corinthians 15:39-40, *The Inclusive Bible*)

As children we were encouraged to sing a hymn written by Carl F. Alexander, 1848, currently altered in the *New Century Hymnal* to read:
All things bright and beautiful, all creatures great and small,
All things wise and wonderful, our dear God made them all,
Each little flower that opens, each little bird that sings,
God made their glowing colors, and made their tiny wings.

My mother had a small telescope with which she used to watch birds. She encouraged me to join her and tried to teach me bird songs, but I resisted. Perhaps it was these early influences which caused me in retirement to seek membership in the National Audubon Society (NAS). I became a beginning "birder" and on the first Easter Sunday morning after retirement, prior to attending an Easter Sunday service of worship, I joined a group on an early morning bird walk. I was photographed by a reporter from the Long Beach (CA) *Press-Telegram*, and to my embarrassment my picture appeared in the Monday edition of the newspaper! Within a couple of months I was enlisted as a member of the board and eventually became president of the El Dorado Audubon Society which held meetings at El Dorado Regional Park, Long Beach, California. I learned that *"The National Audubon Society's mission is to conserve and restore natural ecosystems, focusing on birds, other wildlife, and their habitats for the benefit of humanity and the Earth's biological diversity."* This fits in with my understanding of the action of environmentalists, including many persons of religious faith, in their concern for the preservation and restoration of the ecology of the earth.

My membership in the Long Beach chapter of NAS soon introduced me to the Seal Beach National Wildlife Refuge located on the grounds of the Seal Beach Naval Weapon Station. As a volunteer I was given certification to enter the Refuge to assist with the counting of local bird species. We built and installed platforms for the nesting of the endangered Clapper Rail, cleared a sandy area for nesting California Least Terns, and made a count of Brown Pelicans and Belding's Savannah Sparrows, all species of concern. We also made a count of Red-tailed Hawks, which were listed as threats to the other species. In time I participated in the annual Christmas Bird Counts and the bird census for Los Angeles County Breeding Bird Atlas. Learning of the national concern for both the Eastern and Western Bluebirds, I helped establish a trail of Bluebird houses in El Dorado Park, Long Beach, and since moving to Pilgrim Place in Claremont where I am Conservation Chair for the Pomona Valley Audubon Society, I have established a Bluebird Trail in the Frank G. Bonelli Regional Park in San Dimas with seventeen birdhouses resulting, in the spring and summer of 2007, in fifty Western Bluebird fledglings.

Once in a while I show up at meetings of the Sierra Club, which has enlisted volunteers to assist with the San Gabriel Mountains Campaign, which seeks to enlist volunteers to help clean areas in local mountains where natural habitat has been damaged by humans. Within five years the Sierra Club desires to gain enough public support for political action for Congress to name certain local National Forest Areas as National Wilderness. This would prevent the Forests from being harvested for timber and/or being "developed" with highways, buildings, etc.

"The wilderness that has come to us from the eternity of the past we have the boldness to project into the eternity of the future" - Howard Zahniser concerning the Wilderness Act.

In his book *The Lost Gospel of the Earth*, Tom Hayden writes: *"Our mainstream Judeo-Christian tradition has treated nature primarily as a storehouse of raw materials for our benefit, and as a bottomless container for our waste. The human condition is considered the primary focus of morality, while the tortured condition of nature serves only as a background. Salvation has been promised to the individual, but not to other forms on our planet. The Ten Commandments prohibit adultery but not pollution, demand that we honor our parents but not the earth ... When we worship God above, the earth withers from neglect below. We develop a society where everything from human habits to politics and economics exploits the environment with indifference. Unless the nature of the State is harmonized with the state of Nature, our greed and ignorance will eventually take us beyond the capacity of the very ecosystems that support human existence."* (1-2)

While much of Hayden's statement is true, I do not agree that there is no basis in the Christian Bible for honoring the earth.

In his February 6, 2008 lecture at Pilgrim Place, C. Dean Freudenberger said, "Caring for creation is the only tangible way to express our gratitude to God for our life and for each other during our moment in the mysterious ongoing process of God's creation."

Living at Pilgrim Place in the midst of a community concerned with the issues of war and peace, environmental concerns, and continued growth in theological understanding in the midst of leadership in Process Theology and reading publications of the Jesus Seminar, how could I help but change? I do not yet know where my spiritual journey will lead me but some of the concepts I am considering are included in the following list.

Old	New
Virgin Birth of Jesus	Natural birth of Jesus with human parents
Jesus Christ at once God and Man	Jesus of Nazareth, a human being

". . . Jesus is, for us as Christians, the decisive revelation of what a life full of God looks like. Radically centered in God and filled with the Spirit, he is the decisive disclosure and epiphany of what can be seen of God embodied in a human life. As the Word and Wisdom and Spirit of God become flesh, his life incarnates the character of God, indeed, the passion of God. In him we see God's Passion." (Marcus J. Borg, *The Heart of Christianity*, 88)

Jesus was born in Bethlehem	Probably born in Nazareth
Died for our sins	Died after being tried as a troublemaker

"If Jesus had been only a mystic, healer, and wisdom teacher, he almost certainly would not have been executed. Rather, he was killed because of his politics— because of his passion for God's justice." (Borg, 92)

God, masculine, personal and almighty Ground of Being; Mystery

"The preservation of an appropriate sense of mystery may be the greatest gift that belief in God has to offer our world today. It does not hamper the quest for truth, but tempers that quest with modesty. It does not enervate the search for justice, it tempers it with humility. It does not weaken our capacity to hope, but fills it with patient expectation." (Delwin Brown, "What Does a Progressive Christian Believe about God?" in *The Progressive Christian*, March/April 2008)

Supernatural theism	Panentheism
Eternal life, a gift	Eternal life, a hope
The Bible, infallible, divinely inspired	The Bible, written by people of faith
Prayer changes things, resulting in miracles	Prayer as devotion prepares us for life
Christianity, the only acceptable religion	Many faiths are valid
The Lord's Prayer	Our Common Prayer

The Lord's Prayer (King James Version):
Our Father, who art in heaven, hallowed be thy name.
Thy kingdom come, Thy will be done on earth as it is in heaven.
Give us this day our daily bread.
And forgive us our debts, as we forgive our debtors.
And lead us not into temptation, but deliver us from evil.
For thine is the kingdom, and the power, and the glory, forever.
Amen.

Our Common Prayer in *Prayer at Night's Approaching* by Jim Cotter
(Various revisions of this prayer—which is sometimes listed as
coming from the Maori Anglican Liturgy—have been made,
and the following is one of these revisions.)
Eternal Spirit, Life-Giver, Pain-Bearer, Love-Maker,
Source of all that is and that shall be,
Father and Mother of us all,
Loving God, in whom is heaven:
The hallowing of your name echo through the universe.
The way of your justice be followed by the peoples of the earth.
Your heavenly will be done by all created beings.
Your commonwealth of peace and freedom sustain our hope
and come on earth.
With the bread we need for today feed us.
In the hurts we inflict on one another forgive us.
In times of temptation and test, strengthen us.
From trials too sharp to endure, spare us.
From the grip of all that is evil, free us.
For your reign is in the glory of the power that is love,
Now and for ever. Amen.

"Yes Is a Pleasant Country"[1]
Connie Kimos
May 21, 2008

Rilke, First Duino Elegy: "Who, if I cried, would hear me among the angelic orders . . . ?"

When people ask me what church I belong to, I am hard-pressed to answer. But I have settled on a suitable description: I have a Methodist body with a Greek Orthodox wing and an evangelical wing; or, the roots of me have three branches, but the flower of me is something else grafted.

This is how it all came about. My father was a Greek immigrant, a dashing dandy in spats, vest, fedora, sporting a thin mustache on his upper lip. He must have swept my mother off her feet. She was a naive Swiss girl from the South, waitressing in New York. He was a chef working in the same restaurant, having jumped ship from a Greek freighter in New York harbor. I cannot imagine a more disparate couple. My father was a spirited, gifted, artistic man whose notions of raising his children were brought almost intact from his own upbringing in Turkey and then, after fleeing with his family from Turkish bullets flying over their heads, rescued by a British ship to the island of Lesbos in Asia Minor. My mother was spirited, smart, and musical. She learned to play the piano growing up in her Swiss-German farm family in Elberta in southern Alabama. Her parents and all their 15 children were members of the Christian and Missionary Alliance church. My grandmother took pity on my mother, who stuttered badly. Recognizing that she had musical talent, Grandma procured a piano for her. As a young woman, my mother, having followed her elder sister to New York, worked as a waitress, but she also took singing lessons and joined The People's Chorus; she said they once performed in Carnegie Hall.

We lived in a tiny apartment on the West Side in South Bronx. Life was simple. First of all, my mother considered my brother and me her jewels, and took us for daily outings in our double stroller to a nearby park. My father showed me how to carve a swan from a bar of Ivory soap. My mother taught me not only to read and write at the age of four, but at her knee my first Bible verse: John 3:16: "For God so

---

[1] e. e. cummings.

102

loved the world that he gave his only begotten son, that whosoever believeth in him should not perish but have everlasting life." She would coach me and I would proudly recite it. We attended the nearby Riverside Church on Sunday mornings. She didn't allow us to roller skate or make much noise on Sunday afternoons.

The family moved to Baltimore when I was six. After scouting out churches in the neighborhood my mother chose North Avenue Methodist Church, because it had the best Bible study for her children. We learned our verses, memorized Psalms, and were taught to chant-off all the books of the Bible. Growing into a teen-ager, I expanded and deepened my familiarity with the biblical teachings of God's relations with human beings. Our pastors were topnotch, since our church was one of the elites. Especially, for me, the accounts of Jesus' life had much meaning. I tried my best to live by them.

When I was twelve or so, I earnestly took an oath of Temperance, in Sunday School. That Easter, we had a nice Sunday dinner and my father, feeling festive, wanted us to share a glass of wine. But oh, no, I would not drink. This refusal to join him in a family meal disturbed him to such an extent that life was uncomfortable for us all the rest of the day, and Easter Sunday was spoiled. There were other ways we were often at odds, especially with regard to my opinions, and this caused unpredictable bouts of anger in him and fear in the family. So it went all the way through my growing-up years. At that season of my life, I would often cry, Why God, Why?

Still, every Easter—Greek Easter that is—we would go to bed Saturday earlier than usual, but be woken up around 10:30 or 11:00. Dad would hail a taxi to take us to Greek Church for the Saturday night vigil service. Entering the sanctuary there, I loved the powerful smell of beeswax candles and incense. My father would lift me up to the icon of Christ to kiss it and make the sign of the cross thumb and first two fingers together to touch forehead, heart, right shoulder, left shoulder. In the service, at various points amid the chanting and the choir we would stand or sit at the sound of a sweet tinkling bell. At the end, when the sanctuary lights were put out, we lit our own candle from our neighbor's, and the whole place became ablaze. All this was a Beauty that touched me deeply. We left the church with our lit candles, extinguishing them when we got into the taxi, but we relit them as soon as we got to our apartment building. My father would carefully hold his candle up close to the top of the door frame and make three sooty crosses on the underside, continuing with each doorframe to every room. The crosses would stay for weeks. This ritual continued for 12 years until we moved away from our downtown neighborhood.

During that time, nevertheless, another regular occurrence was our Sunday afternoon hymn-sings at home, gathered around the dinky upright piano my mother saw to it that we would somehow always have. My Swiss grandmother sent us a hymnal from her CMA church, and my mother would play all the favorite hymns she remembered singing in the old days. We all—my two brothers and I, and even my father—would join her, in four-part harmony. The melodies were beautiful, and the sentiments sweet. Precious Hiding Place. No Night There. It Is Well With My Soul. Sweet Peace the Gift of God's Love. Have Thine Own Way Lord. These lodged in my heart, stuck in my right brain, and somehow repaired the emotional violence of my father's outbreaks. Remembered all my life, they visit me still, all unbidden, at odd moments.

At church my mother and I sang in the choir. The director, who had been a trombonist with the Baltimore Symphony, always selected pieces that were classics of the choral genre. I attended Eastern High School, which was one of four schools in Baltimore that were like country day schools. I received an excellent liberal arts education, full of languages, music and literature. I chose to major in music, studying theory and playing violin in the orchestra every day. The whole school sang in parts during assemblies. It was a wonderful, rich life—all in all.

Haiku: "My house having burned to the ground, I now have a better view of the moon."

When I was just going to turn 21, my father died suddenly of a heart attack. I was then able to leave safely for a summer as an employee at the YMCA Conference Center at Silver Bay on Lake George in upper New York State. There I made friends with an extraordinary woman of my own age who introduced me to poems of Rilke and e. e. cummings; music of Mahler; Japanese Haiku; glories of nature under the stars and in the wild mountains. I was utterly changed, from being bound by my father's threats to at last discovering and freely inhabiting my own self.

I quit the teacher's college I had been attending in Baltimore and ventured out on my own to work for a year in order to transfer to a liberal arts college to finish my studies with a BA in French Language and Literature. Following graduation, I taught public high school French for three years. Toward the end of those three years, I was looking for adventure and hoped to teach in another country besides the US. As it happens, I was in church one Sunday when a returned missionary from Africa reported that the Methodist church needed missionary teachers in schools all over the world. I thought surely I might be able to teach French in Africa. Who would have thought, then, that I would end up in Japan?

Rilke, Tenth Duino Elegy: "Someday, emerging at last from this terrifying vision, / may I burst into jubilant praise to assenting Angels! May not even one of the clear struck keys of the heart / fail to respond through alighting on slack or doubtful / or rending strings!"

The summer of 1965, I went to Stony Point New York, for three months' training, along with dozens of other 3s going to Korea, Brazil, Japan, and other countries. Along with our classes in linguistics, cross-cultural psychology and Bible, was a theology course taught by Joe Mathews. He was the director of the Ecumenical Institute in Chicago. He spoke plain, used cuss-words, and demonstrated, or acted out, a radical stance regarding the symbolism of Christ in the church, the Alpha and Omega, the Lamb of God sitting on the throne. He thrilled me with a newly-inspired Christian energy that was not so much an affirmation of going to church, but the intent of Being the Church in the World. I still think of myself as a kind of lay/worker priest.

I arrived in Tokyo that September of 1965, assigned to a half-year of language school, full time every day. The house I lived in was shared by three or four other language school students, one of whom was Pat Patterson. It amazed me to find out she was from Maryland, less than 30 miles from my home in Baltimore, and had graduated from the same Methodist college (Western Maryland—now named McDaniel) a scant five years before me. I was fortunate to have access to her personal library of theology books. Ever the autodidact, I hungrily devoured the ideas of the likes of Barth, Tillich, and Schmemann. And I pondered how I personally should engage in an I-Thou relationship, to what extent I could feel God as in fact the Ground of my Being, what it would mean to Take the Whole World into my Hands as if it were Apple.

Pat had a good friend, the Rev. Yoshio Noro, a Japanese theologian. We went to his small church most every Sunday. He would give us an English précis of his sermons. I took to heart some of his startling notions, such as:

> The desire for security is deadly. Our hands reaching
> out for security will be rejected by Christ . . . The core
> of our human life is chaotic. Man is afraid of this chaos
> so that he makes order in speculation, society,
> organization of justice or ethics. But if you really want
> to love man, you must be chaotic in the core of your life
> . . . Love destroys every system of your making and
> compels you to hear the voice of your neighbor.

So, after my time in Tokyo, I finished out the 1960s in Osaka, seconded to a UCC-related school as English teacher. I "swam" in the Japanese sea, buoyed up by my new learnings, and came to value the ways that the Japanese make sense of the world. I enjoyed living by my own compass. The only really "Christian" thing about me, I suppose, was that I aimed to follow Jesus' example in relating to people. The school asked me to give short morning chapel talks. I acceded, using general examples from Jesus' parables and Robert L. Short's *The Gospel According to Peanuts*. The local church asked me to lead an English Bible class and I used *Good News for Modern Man*, highlighting for discussion those passages that could be applied to society in general, specific issues of ethics or spiritual guidance in the face of Japan's changing mores. As I learned that Japan for hundreds of years was a "network" society, I accepted that and predicted that when their social network was broken, they would need a centering guide. As it was, many had embraced Christian teachings, without daring ultimately to be baptized. To me that was all right, in terms of their culture.

I extended my J-3 term by a year and returned to the US in 1970. I was to attend a returned missionary conference in Greencastle, Indiana. Reaching Baltimore, I was put in touch with an outfit called LAOS, who wanted me to take some materials to the conference. LAOS, originally based in Mississippi as "Layman's Overseas Service," was a broker for Third World work placements for US Christian lay people who wanted to put their skills to good use. Embracing liberation theology, LAOS had no illusions that this work would change the world, but it would certainly change the minds of those who went overseas to "help," and, returning to their home churches, could spread these concepts. Tom and Edna Boone, along with Bob Kochtitzky, had invited both black and white friends to Bible study in their home, but racist neighbors continually threatened, and one night the KKK burned a cross on their front lawn. Fed up at last, they moved LAOS to a hospitable place where they could continue their work, at the Koinonia Foundation Center in the rural outskirts of Baltimore.

Arriving at their office, I noticed the packing boxes and office equipment all askew, and asked if I could help. "Yes!" When I came back from Indiana, I joined the LAOS staff and when, after half a year or so, they moved to Washington, D.C., I went with them. My main work was as the director of the Third World Reader Service, which I helped create. I searched out articles written by Third World people, got permission to reprint, printed them, put them together in a packet and mailed them monthly to subscribers. This was hands-on learning about Liberation Theology and I was an active participant in that political/social justice milieu for two years.

Then Japan beckoned again. In Kyoto, a UCC-related school, Doshisha, needed a teacher for their girls' junior/senior high school. Coincidentally, old friends from New York were living in another part of the city, learning to be practitioners of *chanoyu*—Tea Ceremony. My association with them led to regular book reviews for the Urasenke Tea School's English-language *Chanoyu Quarterly*. Later, leaving the structure of the Board of Global Ministries, I became Associate Editor of the Quarterly, dealing with articles about every aspect of Japanese culture, including architecture, weaving, pottery, tea-growing, cooking, Zen Buddhism, etc. All these relate to the simple act of "heating water, preparing tea, and serving it." This taught me that there is a lot of background for any "simple" act. I am still carrying this idea with me to every part of my life.

A colleague and I compiled a collection of English translations of essays by the Grand Master of Urasenke; we called it *Tea Life, Tea Mind*. It was rich in notions I live by today, adjusting as necessary to my present circumstances.

> We realize humbly our relationship with all that is around us, with the universe. Without this, serving tea becomes an empty and perfunctory form. This pure, simple, and thankful heart . . . comes with a pursuit of self-training and discipline that is akin to the practice of Zen. . . . The Way is wherever people discipline themselves through training. It is not to be found in books. It is through direct experience with our own bodies and not only our intellects that we can attain this state. . . . I make my daily life the place of my practice."

**e. e. cummings: "I'd rather learn from one bird how to sing,
than teach ten thousand stars
how not to dance."**

Those years in the mid-70s I also became friends with Janet Linde and her family. Janet and I found we were companions in search of Things on the Other Side. Transcendental Meditation was one of the saving tools she introduced me to. I attended the occasional classes in Tokyo, guided by Maharishi Mahesh Yogi—yes, the very guru of the Beatles. I learned to quiet my busy mind and "comb" my brain waves by dwelling in a state of scientifically verified spiritual suspension from the physical (well, almost). We initiates met in a community center used by many groups. The day I received my mantra, right next door—to my initial dismay—a loud band was practicing. But when I slipped deep into meditation, I heard nothing. So I learned I could dwell in a kind of magnetic suspension for 20 minutes, and emerge refreshed. I did TM for about 15 years.

During this same period of the mid-70s, one year, I missed going to the annual Japan Women's Conference; Janet went as usual. Elizabeth Kübler-Ross was the speaker. Janet was among a few women who met with her after hours, and saw her off at the train station. Just before the train doors closed, she drew a small book from her purse and gave it to Janet. It was *The Quiet Mind*, a compilation of wise teachings from White Eagle. As Janet told me afterward, it made such an impression on her that she ordered copies from England, and gave me one. Reading the simply-worded yet profound explanations of this Teacher with News from the Other Side, I was moved by the truth of them, with a tearful "of course!" recognition. I felt reassured that the underlying force in each soul's life is Love, which is also Light, and that I have lived many lives in learning my lessons—and that this life is one that I had chosen to be born into! Now all my earlier ignorant straining after understanding of this visible world, this constructed life of mine, sloughed off and I dwelt in a new power: knowing that what we see here is but one side of a coin and the Other Side is just as real and powerful.

In 1984, I attended the first White Eagle Lodge conference in North America, in Colorado. I met the leaders from England and Texas, as well as dozens of adherents, especially from the Long Beach Daughter Lodge. I felt deeply they had something to say to me. I became a member and remain so today, taking on a special work of prayer ritual for the healing of individuals and all of humankind. In

1993, just back from another short stint in Japan, I answered an urging to work at the White Eagle Center for the Americas in Montgomery, Texas. Among my many tasks was the retyping into the computer of White Eagle study materials, from brittle old mimeographed sheets. Fingers flying at the keyboard, over many hours of many days, I absorbed a vast amount of Information from the Other Side, banking it and drawing upon it as I lived, even now, "keeping on keeping on." During my two years there, I took part in ancient rituals of healing prayer in between bouts of manual labor cleaning retreat rooms, filing papers, gardening, sometimes cooking, and playing the keyboard for Sunday services held in the Temple's large round space.

So, in my life I've done this, I've done that; I've thought this and thought that. In the end, it all comes down to Einstein's question: Do you live in a friendly universe or a hostile universe? I surely think I live in a friendly sphere where I am companioned by spirit and by angel, supported by God's loving overseeing of my good. My attitude generally springs to the positive, to my better self, my Christ self. When I leave that plane, and slip into my little self—where negative judgment and "grumblies" drain my energy and poison my heart—I don't like it and am able ever more quickly to get out of it. I live in daily affirmation of "enough-ness." I am thankful for even small physical signs in my surroundings, especially recognizing serendipities such as finding a coin, a nail or a paper clip just when I need it; musical coincidences (such as the time I was playing one of Satie's *Gymnopedies* and, along with a certain low bass note came a jet plane flying overhead with its engine hum on the same note—Duet for Piano and Jet!) or a "chance" encounter with a person who says just the right thing to me, or I to them, and make a helpful connection. I am thankful for my mitochondria, those little eucaryotes that inhabit my body, turning my food and drink into energy for moving my muscles and thinking my thoughts. So, to remind me to employ the wisdom of my heart and of my mind together in my activities, I use as my computer password: *kokoro*, the Japanese word for heart/mind that cannot really be separated, as it is the mind in the heart and the heart in the mind.

I have given up thinking I have control over anything save my own reactions and attitudes. I do still slip into ire, rudeness, thoughtless blurtings, but I quickly catch on, acknowledging that my greatest work is on myself, as I trust God is guiding me to be the best me that God intended. How rich a life!

Haiku: "Simply trust. Do not also the petals fall, just like that?"
I am a minimalist. I tire of great tomes, and prefer haiku or the gems that shine out of longer verbiage. When I try to figure things out only intellectually, it all becomes gobbledygook; I get mired in words. Writing this paper was hard, partly because I've accepted the reality of the ineffable: some things cannot be described. The Tao says it well: "The name that can be named is not The Name."

I am an alchemist, turning base metals into gold. Materialism is not "where it's at" for me, so I am not restricted by Newtonian physics, but plunge further into the subatomic world of neutrons, electrons and quarks. With Wordsworth I aim to see into the life of things; with Blake I hold the world in a grain of sand and eternity in an hour. I understand that thoughts really do affect matter at a deep cellular and subatomic level, as the Hawaiian concept of Ho'oponopono and the pioneering photography of water crystals by Prof. Masaru Emoto have taught me.

Through the pleasant country of Yes, I journey on, to discover treasures that would escape me if my vision were clouded. I pay attention to the beautiful details that make up the whole universe. I smile to recognize that angels and fairies, sprites of the woods and waters and plants, live along with me, doing their work, as I do mine. I can easily recognize old habits of thought, which are as road signs for wide and easy ways, but I have learned to say No to them, and forge ahead with new thought, trails half-hidden, that beckon me. And I, ever adventuring, say: Yes, I'll go there.

I used to cry, "Why, God, why?" But now when Things Change, I murmur in recognition "So this is the Something New you are doing in me!" At times the change may be within, as if the instrument that is me is being tuned by God the Player. Other times it is my entire context, as if the kaleidoscope that is me is being turned by God the Creator. And I rejoice with cummings:

**"i thank You God for most this amazing day . . . for
everything . . . natural . . . infinite . . . yes"**

The Authors
(In alphabetical order)

Charles Bayer has been a pastor, theological professor, newspaper columnist, municipal politician and author, having penned nine books on theology and church life. He has more recently served as a community organizer and advocate of progressive politics and religion. He currently serves as a member of the Board of Directors of "The Institute for American Progressive Democracy," a national think-tank.

Ruth M. Harris, a native Nebraskan, served as a missionary teacher in China from 1947 to 1951, and as field program director for the Student Volunteer Movement, 1954-59. Most of her career was as an executive staff of the United Methodist Board of Global Ministries, first with the Women's Division in student work, 1960-65, and then with the World Division, for University World, 1965-69, and for Global Justice (including urban and rural ministries and youth and young adults), 1977-90. Her work was denominational and ecumenical and involved relations with movement groups around the world. Ruth has a bachelor's degree in school music from Morningside College (Sioux City, Iowa) and a master's degree in international education from Teachers College, Columbia University, New York.

Henry Hayden, a native of Connecticut, graduated from Trinity College in 1939, and Pacific School of Religion in 1944. He spent 10 years in the university chaplaincy at the University of New Mexico and the University of New Hampshire, and 38 years in parish ministry. He served in Guerneville, Fresno, and San Carlos, in California. He was and is deeply committed to the civil rights movement, the farm workers' movement and the gay rights movement. He marched with the Rev. Dr. Martin Luther King, Jr. and César Chávez, and supported the ordination of the first openly gay minister in 1972. He has lived at Pilgrim Place since 1988.

Connie Kimos has been a teacher and a religious seeker most of her life. She graduated from Western Maryland College (now McDaniel) with a B.A. in French and taught it for three years before being sent to Japan by the United Methodist Church as a missionary English teacher in a Christian school in Osaka for four years. This was the start of several sojourns, alternating every few years between Japan and the US at various educational and cultural institutions, as teacher, curriculum consultant, principal, editor, teacher trainer, or staff. Most recently, she worked nine years as program assistant for Urban Ministries and Field Education at the Claremont School of Theology. She entered Pilgrim Place in June 2006. Only semi-retired, she enjoys such work as private secretary, proofreader for international students' graduate theses, and staffer at a holistic health market in Claremont. Continuing interests include cultural linguistics, subatomic physics; organic farming, art and music (including therapeutic harp), and process theology.

Paul Kittlaus is a United Church of Christ minister and has served congregations in Southern California and Wisconsin. He served as Director of an Urban Training Center in Los Angeles, as field staff for Clergy and Laity Concerned About Vietnam and as Director of the UCC Washington, D.C. public policy office. He is now on the board of Progressive Christians Uniting and of the Southern California Ecumenical Council.

Jim Lamb is a Catholic Christian still pursuing the specific implications of peacemaking and justice-making, in our violent, non-communal culture. How should citizens of strong religious faith move beyond good will and good deeds to meaningful transformative action? Early on Jim worked in remote Yucatecan villages. Later, back in Mexico, with wife Joann he co-directed intensive ecumenical programs for North Americans wishing to experience oppressive Latin American realities and indigenous programs to change them. At present he is also learning, with his seven-year-old grandchildren, the vital importance of dialogue, the real meaning of God in our lives, and a lifetime commitment to seeking and speaking truth. (Gabriel Reuter and Isabella Lamb live in the San Francisco Area.)

Richard Moore is a retired ordained minister in the United Church of Christ, now a resident with his spouse, Grace Jones Moore, at Pilgrim Place. He was ordained in 1951 and retired in 1991, but continues to serve as one of the Annuitant Visitors for the UCC by visiting ministers and spouses, lay and ordained, who are currently receiving income from the United Church of Christ Pension Boards.

Pete Nelson is a relatively new resident of Pilgrim Place, having recently completed a little over a year with his bride, Judith Favor. In retrospect his goal during a forty-five-year career in education as an instructor and counselor has been to seek a mutual and reciprocal consciousness and spiritual development. That goal continues.

Peter A. O'Reilly. A medieval scribe wrote, "We indeed are all natives of Ireland, dwelling on the very fringes of the world and the disciples of Peter and Paul." The fact of living at the edge of the great unknown set Peter to wonder at an early age what hidden lands might lie beyond the horizon. So, in 1961, he set out from his native land for the edge of a yet-unknown world, the Pacific Rim, where he has served as a Catholic priest for the past 47 years. His work has been mainly with people in the Greater Los Angeles area, though he has spent some time as a teacher in a local seminary. His great love has always been, and still is, to minister to people on their own spiritual journey and to search with them for what lies beyond.

Pat Patterson. As a missionary teacher in Japan, Pat was exposed to the war experiences of her students in Tokyo, and to atomic bomb survivors in Hiroshima and Nagasaki. During the Vietnam War, she participated in the 50-member US Protestant delegation to the Paris Peace Talks in 1971. Pat became Northeast Asia executive of The United Methodist Board of Global Ministries in New York. Representing US churches, she traveled to Vietnam, including the groundbreaking of the Friendshipment Hospital at My Lai in 1977, and again in 1989 when she went to Cambodia as well. In 1986 she chaired the first NCCCUSA delegation of ten ecumenical colleagues to North Korea and helped draft the NCC's policy paper on "Peace and Reunification on the Korean Peninsula." She has an MA from Drew University, Madison, NJ, in Religion and Literature.

Larry Schulz is a retired ordained minister of the United Church of Christ. He has served in all settings of that denomination; half of his forty-year active ministry was in local churches and the other half in national or regional staff positions. He was executive director of the Council for Christian Social Action of the UCC and has been involved in a wide range of social justice issues. He loves to preach, and in retirement misses that opportunity more than anything else. He has really appreciated the stimulation of the Doing Theology group.

Barbara B. Troxell, born in Brooklyn, New York, a graduate of Swarthmore College and Union Theological Seminary, with additional studies at New College (Edinburgh), the Graduate Theological Union (Berkeley), and Shalem Institute for Spiritual Formation, is a United Methodist clergywoman first ordained in 1958. Prior to retirement at Pilgrim Place in 2002, she had ministered in diverse places as parish pastor, student YWCA executive, United Methodist district superintendent, seminary dean of students (Pacific School of Religion), and seminary faculty member (Garrett-Evangelical). She continues her ministry as spiritual guide, with occasional teaching and retreat leading. She has begun to write her memoirs, with the help both of the "Write Group" and the "Doing Theology" group at Pilgrim Place. She is active in Claremont United Methodist Church, and in peace, justice, and women's movements, including The Grail. She enjoys life with husband Gene Boutilier, singing, traveling, and visiting with family members.

Jean W. Underwood was born in Pomona, California and holds the BA from San Jose State University in California and the MRE from New York Theological Seminary. Her mission was teaching, in the Bible Institute in Chungju and in the Presbyterian Seminary in Kwangju, South Korea (1954-1993).

Printed in the United States
124698LV00004B/1-150/P

9 781600 472428